THE NEW CREATURES

The sequel to
The Captive's Crown

By Olusola Sophia Anyanwu

Copyright © Sophia Anyanwu 2023

The right of Sophia Anyanwu to be identified as author of this work has been asserted by her in accordance with the Copyright, Designs and Patents Act 1988.

All rights reserved.

No part of this publication may be reproduced or transmitted in any form or by any means, electronic or mechanical, including photocopy, recording, or any information storage and retrieval system, without permission in writing from the publisher.

Other books by Olusola Sophia Anyanwu

Stories for Younger Generations
Tales for Younger Generations
Sophia's Fables for Younger Generations
Stories for Older Generations
The Captive's Crown
Turning the Clock Hands Backwards or Anthem
The Confession
The Crown
Their Journey
The Robe

Poetry
Chameleon and other Poems
Sophia's Covid Poetry
Poetry from the Heart

www.olusolasophiaanyanwuauthor.com

*"Therefore, if anyone is in Christ,
he is a new creation:
the old has gone; the new has come."*

2 Corinthians 5:17

*This work is dedicated to my grandchildren:
Olanna, Eberechi, Chima, Chioma,
Chinwe, Chinomso, and Kelechi;
and my future generation by God's grace.*

PREFACE

Who are the New Creatures? You and I, who have been touched by the Lord Jesus and have our minds and lives renewed. How wonderful it all sounds! **But** – how many of us live our outward lives and our inner lives in parallel? Have you heard the tale of the man who had the privilege to board a plane but did not enjoy the luxury of eating the meals? In his ignorance, he did not know that the ticket fare covered his meals on the plane, and so he went hungry.

My purpose in this story is to point out the benefits of enjoying your salvation as a new creature in Jesus Christ, so that you won't be ignorant like the man above. You are no longer tied down by laws and conventions of man. The Holy Spirit of God is there for you when you talk to Him about any issue: love, sex, marriage, children, relationships, conflicts, anger, insecurity, addiction, health, career, and so on.

The characters in this story have been carefully chosen to present some of the issues that pose a conflict for Christians. These are things that can prevent them from enjoying peace and the fullness of their destiny that Lord Jesus gives through the victory of His name.

ACKNOWLEDGEMENTS

My thanks, gratitude and praise go to the Holy Spirit.
Firstly; for inspiration, wisdom, will, strength,
courage, time, and determination,
and secondly; for the successful completion
of this sequel to *The Captive's Crown*.

Thanks also to my editor, Liz Carter, who worked with me patiently, thoroughly, and efficiently with God's grace and strength. It was a great pleasure and joy working with her.

PROLOGUE

Abba had seen the end from the beginning.

He caused all His angels in the entirety of their population in the Heavens and earthly realm to share His pleasure in praise. Every angel understood what Abba had seen. They began to sing and rejoice for those who had received their redemption and salvation. For those who had remained faithful; for those who had won the battle over the flesh; for those who had sacrificed their houses, brothers, sisters, and children to follow Abba; for those who had forsaken their all to follow the right path; for those who had turned their back on all manner of evil; for those who said YES to Jesus and NO to the devil…

These were angels skilled in the playing of every manner of musical instrument known on earth – and those not yet known. This was a symphony; a marriage between the myriads of sounds from the lyre, flute, trumpet, cymbals, strings, harp, tambourine…

So great was their joy that all the spirits of all creation on the Earth praised their maker: creatures in the sea and ocean depths; wild animals and all cattle; small creatures and flying birds; lightning and hail; snow and clouds; stormy winds and rain; fruit trees, shrubs and all cedars; mountains, hills and all valleys; kings of the earth of all nations and people of all gender, age and origin gave praise as they all sang the GREAT ADORATION song:

He – the Omnipresent God
Sees through our eyes
Dazzles with our vision
Works through our minds
Meddles with our thoughts
Creates through our hands
Fiddles with our creation
Moulds through our imagination
Springs with our revelation and
Science comes forth
Emerging with technology
Like dust and ribs
Like the rainbow

He – the Omnipotent God
Creates with words
What science can't fathom
Without the big bang theory
Performs miracles
That technology can't decode
Like the creation in six days
Like the red sea parting
Like the rubble of the Jericho walls
Like the virginal conception of His Son
Like the earthly life of His Son
Like the death of His Son
Like the resurrection of His Son
Reels out numbers mentally
Like the number of seashore sand
Like the number of head hair

Like the number of stars
Like walking on water
Like unmuting the deaf
Like opening sight to the blind
Like enabling the lame
Like transforming impossible to possible
Fought victoriously without an army
Fed five thousand with five sandwiches
Changed era of civilisations
Through death
Through shorter life spans
Through language,
Through a forty day and night flood
Through diversity and religion
Through planned plagues and viruses
Through natural disasters
Through science and technology
Through the power in Jesus Christ's name
Through the blood of Jesus

He – the Omniscient God
Puzzles the brains of scientific geniuses
Defies their reasoning
Undermines their theories
Baffles their intelligence
Mocks their wisdom
Dislodges their assumptions
Deflates their ballooned powers
Mystifies their understanding
Confuses their solutions
Perplexes their musings
Dissatisfies their curiosity
Unwinds their ramblings

Tampers with their findings
Teases with their dissertations
Toys with their notions
Faults their knowledge
Their concept of the Trinity

He – the Almighty Abba God
Blows their feathered confidence
Baffles their curiosity
Unnerves their conclusions
Displays their limitations
Stirs their confusion
Invokes their philosophy
Inspires their quests
Unquenches their thirst
Expands their motivation
Expends their energies
Conquers their conquests
Dissipates their strengths
Authors their talents
Probes their quests
With their carnal minds

As man battles man
to disprove the claims of God
To deny His existence
To pervert His art
To disqualify His abilities
To refute His origins
To unclaim His blessings
To forsake His ways
To destroy His credibility
To mislead generations of mankind

With their poison of
Hatred and sin of unbelief

He – Jesus, God personified, in miracle and marvel
He – God of Revelation
He – God of Redemption
He – Father, Son and Holy Spirit
He – Omnibenevolent God
He – the Creator of life and all
He – God of Heaven and Earth
He – Faithful, Holy God
He – God of Love
He – God of Glory
He – God of Salvation
He – Kings of kings, resurrected King
He – Lord of lords, Lord over death
He – Crown of Victory
He – God of Transcendence and Immanency
He – God of Goodness
He – God of Grace and Graciousness
He – God of wisdom
He – God of Truth
He – God of Praise
He – God of Mercy
He – God of Compassion
He – God of All and Everything

Your breath in every man
Your favour in Your pleasure
Your creation in Your will
Your Holy Spirit is invisible
Tremendously mighty
In stillness, power, and calm

The light of the soul
Enshrouded in Your desire
You hold mystery in your hands
You awe man with Your laughter
Like a mother coos to her amused infant
You keep the mystery of You
Unveiled and unlocked
Till time in eternity with You.

AMEN

CHAPTER 1

Why is your soul cast down?
Psalm 42:5

Come to me, all of you who are weary and carry heavy burdens,
and I will give you rest.
Matthew 11:28

'Eliana, I have been thinking. Let me ask you; do I not please you? What can I do?' Lucas asked in a low tone as he rolled back to his side of their bed, feeling a sense of disappointment and frustration. He gathered his loin cloth, wondering what his wife would say in reply. Something was wrong somewhere. This was not the way he usually knew his wife to respond in their intimacy. She lay beside him on their bed, and through the wan darkness he could see that her eyes were shut. 'Eliana, you heard me?' He turned towards her.

Eliana had heard him. This was so unexpected! She did not understand at first what her husband had meant, and she did not want to ask. It was a delicate time of the night. She had always assumed that Christian married women were to remain silent, saintly, passive, pious and as virtuous as a virgin during the act of coitus, even if they enjoyed the experience. She believed that the more passive a wife was in the marital bed, the more pious she was thought to be in the eyes of God. She imagined that some wives were even fully clothed – at least she was half clothed, wearing a baggy, long-sleeved, knee-length gown, and her hair was free.

She was perplexed. She was no longer living the life of Miriam, the prostitute, who had broken all sexual protocols and taboos with regard to Jewish women and lovemaking. No inhibitions. It was the way of the red trade.

She pondered the matter a few seconds before answering. Keeping quiet meant accepting guilt for something she was still in the dark about. 'My lord, I don't understand you. Are you speaking in parables?' It was a whisper. Everyone had come to realise that Lord Jesus had mostly spoken in parables when He was alive. His words and messages had a double meaning with a hidden message. Surely Lucas had a hidden meaning here?

'No! Why would I speak in parables?' he asked in surprise, moving towards her with an embrace. 'You know we are followers of our Lord and the new life. Eliana,' he sighed, 'I am not speaking in parables. You know very well what I mean, considering we have just made love.'

She suddenly imagined how Zara must have felt over twenty years ago, having not known the Lord. Zara had come to her as Miriam for advice on sex tricks because a client had complained. Now Zara was a new creature in the Lord, and had reverted to her original name, Johanna. Was Johanna also having this problem with her own husband? What did Lucas mean? Was he indirectly complaining? Who could she turn to for help? Was he regretting their reconciliation after ten years apart? Her continued silence must be sending him the wrong signals. She felt panicky, but when she heard herself speak, she sounded completely calm. 'My lord, you know how much I love you. You please me. I hope you are in turn happy with me!'

'Not since Dinah,' he murmured quietly, stroking her long, silky, luxuriously rich hair. Thinking of Dinah, and remembering the way she used to make love with him almost ten years ago, stirred up his passion in a sudden flood of strong currents. Before Eliana could answer, he asked tenderly, 'Or... are you with child, Eliana?'

She noticed his voice was husky with passion and longing. 'No,' she answered softly. *Was she?* Their twin sons had turned a year old a few weeks ago. 'No. It could be that I am still reacting to the pain of the loss of our beloved brother in Christ and remembering Lord Jesus.'

She looked down, knowing she had just lied. *Oh dear! Where was all this leading?* She couldn't help thinking again of Zara, coming to meet her back when she was Miriam. What had Miriam advised Zara then? Did she need that advice now? No, that was not the right way of lovemaking for a married woman and a new creature. Zara and Miriam were prostitutes. She needed to concentrate and remember what she had given to Lucas, all those years ago when she was living in the personality of Dinah, before she was Miriam. She could not focus. Her husband was speaking again.

'You could be pregnant again, you know. We've been living together for twenty-one months now. You remember how it was with our Levi, Logan, and Luke? You conceived immediately I touched you. Maybe this one is female, Eliana.'

Lucas paused. He was hot and hungry for the kind of sexual love Eliana used to give when he knew her in the personality of Dinah, a sinner. Without waiting for her comments, he suddenly drew her closer and thrust himself into her. Squeezing and massaging her buttocks in strong rhythmic waves, he muttered into her hair, telling her how much he loved her. His chin nuzzled her forehead, then her nose, and then he made for her mouth.

Eliana did not realise when she unconsciously slipped into the personality of Dinah. She responded with a deep sigh of pleasure and felt her own desire for her husband rise with equal fervour and heat from the bottom of her stomach's pit to the apex of her heart. She clutched her husband's neck and hungrily kissed him as she released the bottled-up, unbridled passion for just the fourth time in twenty-one months.

It had been so difficult to train her body in this new discipline in line with the new faith as she understood it. Her body had been so pampered, so free to feel things for over twenty years when she lived in the personas and bodies of Reubena, Safirah, Dinah, and Miriam. Freedom of love was sweet. As her body slipped deeper into its old mode, the heat of her passion engulfed her, bursting out with all her suppressed feelings and yearning for intimacy. She heard herself weeping in response to ecstasy as she told her husband how much she loved him and wished this moment would never end...

Afterwards, though, she quickly reverted to 'holy' Eliana, with feelings of guilt and remorse assailing her on all sides. She trembled when two new assailants joined her adversaries: shame and fear. She felt defeated and humiliated, even worse than the way she had felt fourteen months ago, when, wearing just a slip of a transparent negligee, her hair all loose and her taut nipples peeping through the thin material, she had been expecting Josef, a client who had become a friend. However, when she opened the door, there stood Rachel, her 'new' mother, with Mother Abigail and Mother Ahuva. She was mortified and ashamed, and even now clearly recalled the strong scent from her heady perfume pervading the nostrils of her visitors, leaving them in no doubt as to her true intentions.

Oh my God, she thought now. *What have I done? God, what are you thinking about me now? Look into my heart. I am so sorry. And Lucas? What is he thinking right now about me?*

The answer came immediately. Lucas grabbed her trembling body, planted a kiss on her forehead and muttered, 'Now I know my Dinah has come back to me.'

Soon he was sleeping the deep sleep of the contented.

His answer did not restore her peace.

Dinah! Did he just call me Dinah? Why? I don't wish to remember the past. The old ways. I hope Lucas is not like Asher, my father, deep inside. Surely, he knows that my new faith means I am dead to the old way of life? I know I just slipped back into the old ways. Lucas too must have slipped back, but I know I did not do so deliberately. Did he mean to call me Dinah, or was this in error? This is the first time; I will wait and see if it happens a second time. I will tell him to never call me by that name again!

Eliana was certain that Lucas was like Kazim – a rich client of her old self as Miriam, the prostitute. Kazim was married yet he regularly visited *Miriam's House of Pleasures*. Lucas had tasted the forbidden fruit. His eyes were open. He had never been into a harlot's den, like Kazim, to get initiated; instead, Dinah, a harlot, had come into his own den and initiated him into the wild pleasures of the red lady. His flesh had been hungry for exotic pleasures, which only the likes of Dinah and Miriam could provide. Could this be the reason why Lucas had accepted her back? Or was he going to be temped like Kazim to go and look for 'exotic pleasures' outside the home? Here she was, training her body to be disciplined, trying to subdue the old ways of her flesh so that the new would stay for good.

This could not continue. *There is no use keeping this to myself. I'll first discuss it with…*

Her thoughts came to a pause. Whom could she confide in? It had to be someone who would not judge her: someone who would not have any doubt that she was not the old creature hiding under the skin of the new creature; someone who would not reason that she had backslidden or that she was still of the old life and had not killed her fleshly desires because they were too sweet to let go. Whom could she turn to? The Centre did not seem to have mothers one could turn to. She remembered a few occasions when mothers were approached, and they would themselves go and seek counsel from the disciples of the Lord. Even Mother Mary would talk to Lord Jesus and His disciples. Now Lord Jesus was gone, and within this last year after His death most of his followers had faced persecution. Some of his devoted disciples had been killed! Eliana felt tears come to her eyes. She would have to carry this burden alone and hope she and Lucas did not slip back into the former ways of the flesh.

She wondered to herself. Could she possibly be the mother who changed an old, erroneous belief – that sex should solely be for procreation and not for the pleasure of married women? What a misconception. She could start a counsel group for married women. She would let them know that sex should be enjoyed by married women. They should feel free in their natural desires and to enjoy what God provided. After all, why did Solomon have to marry 700 wives and 300 concubines until he found true love in the Shulamite woman?

If she spoke to Razi about this, would Razi become more protective of her husband Josef in order to protect him from her? What of Johanna? Would Johanna understand and not mock her or laugh behind her back with Mother Abigail? If she spoke to her own mother, Rachel, would that be confirming her father's attitude towards her? Besides, her mother had never revisited that shameful incident when she found Eliana dressed as a prostitute, seemingly waiting for a client. Her mind went to her father,

Asher, and she sighed. This problem was her cross to bear for now. She tried to talk to Abba but couldn't find words.

It was the first crow of the early cockerel that sent her into a light sleep.

That same night, in another area a walking distance from Eliana's house, another woman's mind was heavily occupied and sleep kept far at bay.

Dawn came suddenly, heralded by the cock crowing. Rachel knew she had not slept well. This was not the first time; it was, in fact, becoming a pattern. Most nights she would listen to her husband snore in his sleep beside her. This morning, though, she didn't realise that her husband, Asher, was also wide awake and ruminating on thoughts similar to hers. A lot of things weren't right.

Rachel kept her mind awake thinking of her life now that she was reconciled with her husband. After how many years? Eliana's age was the yardstick: thirty years! She ought to be happy and excited considering how, in the space of under two years, she had found her daughter, Eliana; and she had been reconciled to Asher, her husband. Her family had grown. Asher had another family from before; he had married a woman named Tisha, who had died two years earlier. She had given him two sons: Dan and Tobiah. They were married, but Dan, his wife Keziah, and their three daughters lived in the same house with Asher and Rachel. Dan was very much like his father: a traditional Jew, who did not accept Jesus as the Messiah.

That was not why Rachel was unhappy, though. Hers was not the only home or family with such a structure. Her unhappiness stemmed from two facts. Firstly, Asher did not want to hear the name of Lord Jesus in his home, and so she was not free to enjoy her new faith. Secondly, he did not share in the excitement of being reconciled to their daughter, Eliana. To Asher, Rachel discerned, their daughter was an outcast to the family because she had been a prostitute. He did not say this openly, but his actions towards Eliana were rather cool. Rachel thought that by now there would have been a change, but Asher never visited Eliana, even when the twins were born. It was always Eliana and Lucas visiting them, but they had not visited in over six months.

Whenever Rachel visited her daughter, Asher was distant towards her almost to the point of malice. Last month he had accused her of being over imaginative, blaming her faith. Anything she did 'wrong' was attributed to her faith.

As if her practice of the new way of life as taught by Lord Jesus was a taboo!

Rachel had travelled to visit Mother Mary to seek her counsel on the matter. Mother Mary had in turn prayed for her and assured her that it would be best to hear what the rest of the brethren thought on the issue. It was a complex situation. She didn't want to break up her marriage. At the same time, she wished to visit the Believers' Centre again and enjoy the fellowship of the brethren. Mother Mary had promised to send word to her through a trusted disciple.

Rachel thought about her last visit to Mother Mary, two months ago on a cool breezy afternoon, with a group of women who sat together to talk and pray.

'Can you believe Asher begrudging my excitement over Logan and Luke because he is not happy about my new faith?' Rachel said to her listeners, her forehead creased with concern.

Mother Mary sighed, but Mother Ahuva and Mother Tamar shrieked loudly in unbelieving shock. 'Should Asher not be pleased to have two new grandsons and be proud of their progress and their development?' Mother Tamar asked.

'How did you express the arrival of their birth?' Mother Ahuva wanted to know.

Rachel was too angry to give an answer to her question. All the women began to talk at once, asking questions which became rhetorical when answers were not provided. Indeed, the problem seemed magnified.

'Shouldn't there be unity in the family?' Mother Tamar asked. 'Parents should stay together in love. If Rachel leaves, can she have victory over the devil? Won't demons come in and spoil things and the love you have for your husband?'

'Where there is no fellowship, there is no spiritual growth in your mind. Will you be happy, Rachel?' Mother Mary asked.

'In fact,' Mother Ahuva pointed out, 'if there is no common interest between Asher and Rachel, true love will be unattainable. And, if there is a threat to the unity of the family, the marriage and their living in the peace of God, can Rachel be focused on her new faith?'

'I agree with Tamar about promoting family unity and peace. I also remember that Lord Jesus used to depart from a village or town that did not want to hear Him. He never forced His will or love on anyone who would not accept it,' Mother Mary added quietly.

'Then let her leave the marriage! How can Asher be redeemed if he won't let anyone pray for him or allow Rachel to enjoy a relationship with brethren and her daughter? How can she enjoy the package of salvation? See how she is losing weight and looking so unhappy.'

Rachel covered her eyes in grief, the tears leaking through her fingers, and didn't even look up to see who this last speaker was.

Eventually, Mother Mary stated that it would be better to seek counsel from one of the Lord's disciples, and Eliana returned home with hope. At least there had been an argument weighing the pros and the cons, she thought. Her spiritual and emotional wellbeing were being considered.

She began to nurse the hope of going to live with Eliana and resuming her life in fellowship with the brethren at the Centre. But, after two months had gone by, she began to wonder why it was taking so long to get feedback on her case.

Then, just the evening before, someone had visited her at a very timely moment. Asher had just stepped out with Dan, his younger son. It was something to do with receiving a parcel from Tobiah and his wife, Biliah.

Rachel was in the kitchen, helping with the evening meal along with Asher's three granddaughters. Their mother, Keziah, was heavy with a fourth. Everyone hoped it would be a son.

There was a knock at the door. A Sister Naomi identified herself, and Rachel was taken aback by her young age. *A youth*? Youths were generally known to be indifferent to other people's problems; rash, quick to judge, and often belittling. The opposite of wisdom! Rachel herself experienced this in her home. Dan was only too happy to tell her what he wanted her to hear and not the other way round. Just the other day, he had asked her who she thought she was to talk to him about morals.

This lady was even younger than twenty-six-year-old Keziah! Rachel had been expecting a matronly personality: a mother of the new faith; a mature woman who would keep confidence and not give rejection but understanding. On meeting Sister Naomi, she instantly put her walls up. She smiled, perking herself up to reflect confidence and strength and to wear the righteous look of a mother in the church and the new faith.

'Good evening, Mother Rachel,' the girl said.

'Good evening, my good daughter,' Rachel replied, bracing herself to offer prayer, counsel or encouragement to the younger woman.

They made their way to the private chamber room used for important meetings and settled down. 'Mother Mary said to find you,' Sister Naomi said. 'So, I am here to give you a message and encourage you on the matter you left with her two months ago. By the grace of God and the power of the Holy Spirit, you will receive divine help, comfort and peace.'

Rachel struggled to hide her disappointment at seeing that one so young had been elected to give the feedback and encourage her.

Naomi chatted on. 'Mother Mary and the brethren send their greetings and hope I find you well.'

'I am well, thank you. How is she and all the brethren there?'

'Oh, by God's grace, it is well with them all.'

Then a pause, heavy with silence, as if Naomi was finding a way to break in so conversation could flow between them.

'I have just thanked God for His faithfulness,' she said at last. 'Before my trip here, I prayed to God to create the perfect atmosphere and privacy for our meeting. Just as I was approaching your home, I saw Father Asher and his son, Dan, on their way out. This is a divine appointment. Father Asher said they had a parcel to collect from Tobiah.' Rachel watched Naomi unconsciously admire the modest room with approving eyes. 'So, by God's grace, we have some precious time to share together.'

'Oh, yes,' Rachel confirmed, 'Tobiah is my younger stepson. He helps with his wife's business, as they have a baby son.'

'That is wisdom,' Naomi replied with a sweet smile. Then she launched straight into prayer. *'God, please give me the right words at the right opportunity and prepare Mother Rachel's heart to receive Your counsel through me. Amen.'*

'Amen,' Rachel said.

'How are your family members here?' Naomi asked, kindness colouring her eyes.

'Very well, Naomi, thank you. I see you already know the names of my family members prior to meeting me! Dan's three daughters are busy in the kitchen, as Keziah their mother is heavy. So, I spend lots of my spare time knitting baby clothing when not engaged with the housework or selling things in my daughter's shop.'

'Knitting used to be my lovely pastime before I became engaged in the work of the Lord at the Believers' Centre.'

'What kind of work?'

'Oh, counselling, praying, and encouraging brethren in their new faith. But what I enjoy most is listening to testimonies and singing hymns with the brethren.'

'That is exactly what I am missing,' Rachel said sadly. 'Oh, it is so painful to be cut off from a life that gave me so much satisfaction and fulfilment.' A sharp pain cut at her throat as she said these words.

'Why have you stopped?' Naomi asked her, a slight frown creasing her young face.

'Asher no longer approves of my going to the Centre. I used to go just once every two weeks. But now, that has stopped.'

'Any reasons, Mother?'

Rachel shrugged. 'He just doesn't approve.'

'How long were you usually away for?'

'Just three hours.'

'Ah, it must have been so blissful! Ours is less than two hours; still, I do not stay that long because my father is aged and disabled and needs me around him. Don't worry, Mother Rachel. God has something more rewarding than you can imagine. God will bring you into a new season and will pay you back for your obedience to your husband. It is God to whom you have shown loyalty. God will make up for all the time lost and restore your joy.'

'Amen. That is exactly what I want!' Rachel burst out, feeling sparks of renewed hope refreshing her soul. This young lady reminded her of Razilla, a former prostitute. 'But only a touch from Lord Jesus can change Asher's heart,' she remarked gloomily.

'Through His Holy Spirit who is available for us,' Naomi replied. 'When did you last ask your husband's permission?'

'It's been a very long while now, as he categorically ordered me to stop. As a good wife should, I obeyed without any argument, but now I am totally fed up with the situation. I think my relationship with God is more important than anything else in my life.'

Naomi nodded. 'True. After we have prayed for God's intervention to soften his heart and for favour on the matter, you can ask him again. You could consider the idea of starting a fellowship in your home here with a few people and no longer than an hour to share testimonies, sing, and pray. Just ask, because what God opens, no man can shut. Lord Jesus is alive forever, don't forget. Nothing in your life and family is beyond His touch and help. Continue to keep your focus on God and the peace and grace of God to persevere will be multiplied to you.'

'Amen. Thank you! I love the wonderful suggestion about the fellowship. I could start with my own family here; with my neighbours! You really are God-sent. I feel very hopeful.'

'Good. Let us pray on it.' Naomi bowed her head. *'Dear God, You softened Pharaoh's heart and granted Moses favour. Moses was successful and led Your people to worship You in the wilderness. I now ask in the name of Jesus Your son and our Lord to soften Asher's heart. Let Mother Rachel continue to enjoy the fellowship of the brethren again. Please permit that this home will also be a centre for the gathering of Your people to experience Your love, peace and unity and to receive deliverance and salvation as they glorify you in the name of Lord Jesus Christ. Amen.'*

Rachel smiled. 'AMEN! Thank you so much, my daughter, Naomi.' That prayer had voiced her unspoken wishes, her dreams, and the desires of her heart. *Oh God, how awesome and excellent You are. You love me so, so much!* 'Now… enough of me and my worries. Let us talk about you. Iron sharpens iron, as they say. In what area of your life do you need the touch of God?'

But Naomi stood up instead, as the aroma of basil from the kitchen wove through the house and into their noses. She began to move very slowly towards the door. 'I must be on my way now, or my father will become anxious.'

'You must forgive my manners. Have a drink, at least, while we talk about you. Please.'

'Mother, just pray that my father, Samson, will receive healing and that I will be blessed with a man of faith as my husband.'

'That is easy for our God. You will be a priority in my prayers this night to Lord Jesus.' Rachel embraced Naomi, and on impulse said, 'Also… forgive me, my dear daughter, for despising your youth when I first heard why you were here. God has also taught me a lesson today.'

Naomi smiled sweetly as she followed Rachel to the door. 'God loves you,' she said in parting.

Reflecting on Naomi's visit reminded Rachel of the powerful prayer that they had both prayed last evening about God softening the heart of Pharaoh. God alone knew how He would do it, just as He had parted the Red Sea for His people to cross over to Canaan – the Promised Land. *Please, God, answer every request made by Sister Naomi this evening, and don't forget to heal*

Father Samson, and please find a good husband who believes in Lord Jesus for dear Naomi. Bless them with...

Sleep took over quickly, but Abba God had heard her prayers – the spoken and the unspoken desires of her heart. Abba at that very moment was dispatching His angels in every direction to make the prayers of all the New Creatures come to pass.

That same early dawn, in the same house, same room and same bed, Father Asher was also reflecting on some incidents that had happened the day before. The same cock crow that had awakened his wife had also woken him. These days when he was lying in bed awake, he often contemplated the new faith which seemed like a fever infecting everyone in all the villages in Jerusalem City and its environs. His family was no exception. Even his beloved son Dan seemed to be softening and leaning towards it; Rachel's influence, no doubt. He enjoyed a unique relationship with Dan. They were more like twin brothers in looks and closeness; people often remarked on it. Tobiah took more after Tisha, whom Asher had loved very much. She came into his life when he had needed a mother, friend, wife, and soulmate all wrapped into one. When tetanus took her from him, he did not seek another wife; Dan had stepped in to help. They were open to each other, though Asher knew Dan was aware that he hid the entire truth of why he had put away his wife and daughter, Rachel and Eliana, thirty years ago.

Deep down in his heart, Asher secretly suspected that Tobiah was jealous of his relationship with Dan, and that this had driven him to male prostitution. He shuddered in the darkness. Tobiah had sinned against Heaven and him. Abomination! But he was very grateful and thankful to God for restoring Tobiah to goodness in matters of sexuality, as expected of men in their Jewish faith. Why was Dan softening? Was it Tobiah's involvement with the new faith? Probably. He remembered their outing last night to see Tobiah and recalled their conversation regarding the new faith and the woman who had visited Rachel.

'Father, who is that lady?' Dan had asked as they left, glancing backwards. 'I have never set eyes on her, but she seems not to be a stranger to our home – as if she has visited it before.'

'I don't know her, son. I was just about to ask you if she is a friend to Keziah.' His son's puzzled expression told him otherwise.

'But the way you opened up to her about our purposed trip assured me you knew her, Dad,' replied Dan, looking as surprised as his father.

'Don't look at me as if to make me guilty,' Asher said in an upbeat tone. 'I just assumed she was known to Keziah or Rachel, and don't forget the culture of embracing strangers with warmth and courtesy.'

'Talking about Mother Rachel, Father, what is it you really have against the new faith or Lord Jesus? I *really* want to understand.'

'Alright.' He kept quiet for several seconds, then said, 'I met Jesus for the first time about two years ago. I was selling my goods in the temple; you know – the usual doves, for temple sacrifice. Do you know He came in like one possessed and began upsetting everyone's business? I was badly affected. As He stepped into the temple that Thursday evening, he kicked my cage of birds down. It broke, and all my pigeons and doves flew out. I lost so much money...'

'But, surely, are you not glad the Lord restored your long missing wife and daughter to you? That should compensate for any grudge you have against Him. Mother Rachel and Eliana have brought blessings into our family which they attribute to the Lord. He restored Tobiah too!'

Asher frowned. 'Whose side are you on now? Have you been fooled by your half-sister's wealth through harlotry? Can't you see it is a means to gain entrance into our hearts and poison us with the new faith?'

'Would there be anything wrong in embracing the benefits of this new faith brought by Rabbi Jesus, at least?' Dan asked.

'To what purpose? Rabbi Jesus had the power to defeat our enemies – the Romans – and He didn't. He just let himself get killed! I cannot bring myself to reconcile with that.'

'Eliana said she heard Him predict his death the evening she met Him for the first time at Matthew's party. Tobiah and Biliah heard Him too.'

Silence.

'Father?'

Silence.

'Alright, then,' Asher finally said, 'this parcel we are going to collect: this is about the third time. Do you know who our mysterious benefactor is?' He knew he had changed the topic deliberately. He suddenly could not understand his animosity towards Eliana and Rachel.

'I think I know. It is part of our embracing the benefits of the new faith. Can you accept that?' Dan asked.

'I don't see it that way. If it is from Eliana, as I suspect it is, she is just abiding by her moral duty to respect and show honour to her parents as God commanded in the Ten Commandments through Moses.'

'Father, do I have a moral duty to respect and show honour to my siblings?'

Asher remained silent, then, a few moments later, replied, 'Of course, as long as you remain faithful to Jehovah.'

'Are all our kinsmen, relatives, including Eliana and Mother Rachel, unfaithful to Jehovah for believing that Rabbi Jesus is the Son of God?'

'What do you think?'

'Me? Er, truthfully, I'm sometimes convinced and sometimes confused. All I know is that anyone who encourages people to understand God's ways better or get closer to Him can't be against Him or wish me evil. Father, I have witnessed Lord Jesus doing good to people. He loved everyone. I saw people He had healed and touched. *We* have seen what He did for Tobiah. That is a great miracle, father, which I cannot deny.'

'That is sensible,' Asher agreed. 'What then is your confusion?'

'The same as yours: that Jesus claimed to be the Anointed One. Then there's the rumour that his mother conceived him before she was married to her husband, Joseph.' Seeing his father shake his head, he was encouraged to speak further. 'Moreover, what about all that talk that Jesus came back to life three days after he was crucified! Why did he allow himself to be killed if he was just going to come back to life three days later?' He shrugged his shoulders. 'Anything else you could add, Father?'

'Yes. I don't understand his authority to forgive fellow human beings their sins and his assertion that the way to the Kingdom of God is through him.'

His son nodded in agreement. 'What is *your* conviction about the new faith, Father?'

Asher thought for a moment. 'The miracles Jesus performed are way beyond this world. You will agree with me. Everyone agrees too that God was definitely with him. Look at how Rachel was healed and forgave me for the past and returned with Eliana to our family. These are miracles!'

Dan nodded. 'Yes, and don't forget what Tobiah witnessed and told us.'

'Please, son, remind me.'

'Well, Tobiah was among a group of friends, and they were lamenting bitterly about how Jesus had been abandoned in his time of need and wondering where all the thousands of people Jesus had touched physically and spiritually were. Father, he said they suddenly saw Jesus in front of them and he had told them, *'Be at peace.'* Then He *disappeared!* So, Father, if the miracles of Jesus give you some conviction, then please allow Mother Rachel and other family members to visit Eliana. We owe this duty as family members. After all, despite your silent hostility, she has been faithful as a daughter in sending parcels without fail.'

Seeing his father was not answering, Dan changed the topic. 'Father... on our way back, please tell me more about your past pain and the genesis of your grudge against Mother Rachel and Eliana.'

Asher looked at him, his eyes dark with sadness. 'I will, if you will forgive me the evil I did to them. Do you promise?'

'Only on two grounds. Firstly, whatever caused you pain, let it go so that you will no longer have bitterness against them. Secondly, *please* approve Mother Rachel's resuming fellowship at the Centre.'

Asher paused for a minute, then said, 'Alright. Agreed. I will be more lenient... look, your brother is outside, as if he was expecting us!'

As he thought back over their conversation, Asher now found his mind beginning to close down in the weariness of dawn. Before he dozed off, he settled in his heart that he would not be a stumbling block to Rachel; she had suffered enough in the past. Dan had made him feel so evil for what he had done to his wife and child in the past and for how he was still treating them now. He could now see it was wrong of him to have blamed the fate of the two sons he lost in Ramah three decades or so ago on Eliana. It wasn't baby Eliana's fault that she had cried because of her ill health and that her wailing had attracted the Roman soldiers to their dwelling. Perhaps that was just a coincidence. It wasn't her fault they had killed his two little boys.

God had given him two more, and they were so close to his heart. And Rachel? She had been sorrowing in grief at the loss of her two tiny sons, both under the age of two years, at the command of the evil Herod. Both had been murdered in one day before her very sight and, eventually, this had led to her breaking down mentally. *How could I ever have got tired of caring for her? How could I have abandoned her?* He heard the accusation and condemnation in Dan's voice on their way back home this last evening, and it spoke to him. He decided he would make it up to Rachel by attending the Centre now and again. He would start next Friday. This would definitely make her happy, and maybe he could also make his peace there with his daughter, Eliana. After all, if he could accept his own son Tobiah and forgive him for his past detestable life of prostitution, then he could do the same for his daughter. Beautiful Eliana.

He fell into a fitful sleep.

One of the angels Abba named *Wisdom* communicated His thoughts to bless people on Earth:

Wisdom: Whatever is true, whatever is noble, whatever is right, whatever is pure, whatever is lovely, whatever is admirable; if anything is excellent or praiseworthy – think about such things.

Wisdom: Do you see a person skilled in their work? They will stand before kings and great men.

Wisdom: A man's gifts make room for him.

CHAPTER 2

The truth shall set you free.
John 8:31

Show me Your ways, O Lord, teach me Your paths;
guide me in Your truth and teach me,
for You are my Saviour,
and my hope is in You all day long.
Psalm 25:31

'Father Lucas! Where is your mind?'

Lucas was startled, abruptly called away from his deep thoughts about how he had got himself back into a marriage God had delivered him from…

'If this is what marriage does to a guy, I'd better hold fast to my bachelorhood!' remarked Simeon the Junior, his young co-worker and employee. 'I have been watching you for some time now, not just today. I thought you should be amongst the happiest men on Earth.'

Lucas sighed and kept his silence. *Should I be very happy?* 'I don't understand what you are getting at.' His face relayed his doubts.

They were both in the office, cross-checking the list of customers who had hired Lucas's boats for the next day, the drivers, the destinations, and the money collected.

'I mean, you are now married but still look gloomy and lost sometimes. Marriage has not brought you that sparkle,' Simeon said.

'What can I say?' Lucas pushed his hair back. 'So, you have been observing me to gauge what married life is like. Is that it?' He mopped sweat from his brows. The air in the office was stifling.

'Sort of. I am puzzled. You have a good business going, you're in good health, you have sons and a very beautiful wife,' Simeon said sincerely.

'Have you met my wife, Simeon?' *That is a mistake. Why have I asked that question? Do I want to be broken-hearted a second time?*

'No, I have not.'

'How do you know she is beautiful, then?' Lucas asked, unable to stop the words coming.

'Because you wouldn't marry an ugly one, would you?'

Lucas laughed, relieved, and Simeon laughed with him. It had just been an innocent remark. He was always alert and on edge when anyone referred to his wife. He lived in dread that one of her clients from her past life would meet him and taunt him. It was because of this that he did not feel free to go out with her anywhere. Her beauty made male heads turn, and he wasn't sure whose head might belong to a former client.

'Besides,' Simeon continued, 'I heard God did something so wonderful for you.'

'You said you heard? From whom?'

'First from my father and then my neighbour, who goes to the Centre and has been trying to persuade me to go. I remembered you used to go, and I asked if he knew you and he did. Do you know Abel?'

'Probably. What else did he say?'

'He asked why you had stopped coming to the Centre. Have you stopped?'

'Not exactly, but I stay back most times to help my wife with our twins. What else did he say?'

'He said you had an amazing testimony – whatever that means! And that I should ask you. And if I knew, I would surely want to come to the Centre! I knew he was one of those Jews following that new faith, and I lost interest and dismissed him. Did I do right, Lucas?'

'You did right.'

As Lucas made his way home, he felt guilty about the way he had answered Simeon. He felt so bad about putting someone off the right path – and because of what? It was very difficult for him to share his own testimony with other Jews who were not believers of the new faith. It meant talking about how his wife was a harlot in Jerusalem and Samaria for over twenty years, and then revealing how she had changed her name, travelled to Sidon and found her way into his house as a wife pretending to be a virtuous lady. When she was found out, she ran away, and he was reconciled to her ten years later. She had met Lord Jesus, and the old things had passed away; she was now 'a new creature'.

Lucas never shared his testimony in that way. Yes, he mentioned a misunderstanding with his wife, and that they had been separated. Due to his ill health, he had not been able to live with his son. Lord Jesus healed him, and he was back with his family.

That was how he liked to tell it, but some overzealous brethren had spilled it all out. Even Eliana, like him, was a private individual and never gave anyone the encouragement to hear the testimony from her own mouth. All she had shared was that she had been separated from her birth parents and family and estranged from her husband and family, but God had brought her back into reconciliation with them all. Did that sound so amazing?

He wondered.

It was his private life, and he did not like that at the Centre, it was the main topic. The big testimony of all ages, mentioned to every newcomer; used as an evangelistic tool to those outside the new faith. How many times had he been stopped to recount the testimony or asked how it felt to live with a former 'sinner'? It was great that they had twins, and he used this excuse to stop attending fellowship at the Centre. He was conscious of the damp and heavy mood which was becoming an attachment, fastened onto his daily life and even his temperament. What was the difference between his life now in Jerusalem and his life in Sidon after Dinah had left him? The same restlessness, dissatisfaction and constant fear had set in. Should he regret reconciling with Eliana? When he heard that she had been reformed and touched by the Master, it seemed all so new, exciting, and hopeful. Surrounded by all the brethren, they felt secure in their small world of believers.

Outside that world, they were met with challenges.

You married a harlot? How do you feel when her former clients greet her? What if some of her clients had been friends of yours – how do you cope? Why were some people keeping their distance from him? Were they former clients or just against the new faith? He had gladly left Sidon because his friend Aaron had broadcasted to all and sundry the story of the beautiful harlot who had masked as an innocent bride and became his wife.

Lucas remembered how, when they had first married, he had wondered at her sexual prowess, and how he had not questioned this, although somewhere inside he must have known she was not a virgin. He had just been very satisfied with her awesome beauty and her role as a wife and a mother.

Even when he returned to Sidon immediately after the reconciliation, his dear friend Sosthenes voiced his doubts. Had Lucas sacrificed his future happiness by going back to Eliana? Should he have gone ahead with a different life as soon as Levi, his son, returned? What kind of future awaited Levi? Now Lucas was worried that as long as they stayed in Jerusalem, people would tell their offspring about them, and it would be told to generations to come how his children were mothered by a harlot.

Lucas thought about how this had happened to Rahab, the redeemed harlot of Jericho, and her husband Salmon, a devoted, faithful Jew. Their son, Boaz, grew up sidelined by other Jews. It had affected his chances of getting a Jewish bride, even though he was handsome and rich. It was not until he was well over fifty that he had married Ruth, who was not Jewish. Salmon's bloodline got tainted when he married outside the faith and, worse, to a harlot. Boaz was known as the son of a harlot – what a near parallel. And so too were his children. They would probably marry foreigners, or children of harlots, or maybe people outside their faith. What had he done? His own side of the family did not support Eliana, apart from his sister, Rebecca. They had misunderstood his grief all those years. *'We thought you were sad for Levi. You really love that harlot?'*

And now that he had his wife back, she was afraid to love him in that way she had when she had masked as Dinah. Over their twenty-one months of marriage, Eliana had 'sexually slipped' thrice, and was immediately remorseful. He felt her tension each time he lay with her. He had ignored the world's condemnation and criticism to be with her, partly because of the physical love he had thoroughly enjoyed with her and yearned for when he lost her. He had sacrificed his own reputation, the support of his family, and a lot more, but she scored extremely high marks as a wife and a mother, just like the perfect proverbial wife Solomon had spoken of.

He might have to move to another town. Was that a solution? But take Aaron, for example: he had been a client from her past when she had masked herself as Safirah at Samaria. What was the guarantee that such a thing would not happen if they moved to another town? Eliana had had four lives as a harlot in four different towns! They would need to have a serious conversation about the way forward.

For now, though, his life was becoming a drag. He constantly worried about the future, and this prevented him from achieving his highest potential at work. Even Simeon the Junior, his colleague, had noticed and was perplexed. But with whom could he talk about it all?

It was with this heaviness of heart that he arrived home almost an hour later. He saw his eldest son, Levi, helping to tidy up. Eliana was probably busy putting their one-year-old twins to bed. She would feed them, bathe them, and lie in bed with them till they both fell asleep. Then she would help Levi finish up whatever was left to be done before she paid him any attention. By then, he was washed up and ready for the evening meal.

Eliana lay awake later that night. Her husband was obviously not in the mood to touch her. This had been a pattern for two months now. Should she feel relieved or anxious? He had returned home in a sour mood. This had also become a habit, especially since she had refused to be Dinah in bed. After that last night of being Dinah, she went quickly back to herself, Eliana, and she discerned that Lucas was thoroughly unhappy about this. His keeping away from her each night was his way of communicating his displeasure. Even now, she knew he was awake and unhappy. Yet she wondered if their sexual life was the real reason. Lucas was a believer of the new faith, who now understood the concept of the new creature; the idea of the need of the Spirit as opposed to the desires of the flesh. She felt his discontent had to do more with her past life as a prostitute. She had discerned his discomfort at fellowship when their testimony was given to the glory of God, and sensed his tension when she was called out to testify how she had become a new creature. Even then, she had not delved into her past. One of the mothers there had already done that.

She remembered sharing her encounter with Lord Jesus at Matthew's party and how the Lord had ministered to her soul and delivered her. She told how she had felt so grateful and wanted to give all she had to Lord Jesus, and so she had anointed His feet with nard perfume, using her hair to dry them. People had gasped. Nard was worth a fortune to most people. Had she come across as wasteful or pompous? Could that be the issue? She told Lucas about how a lot of people had complained about the waste of the perfume, which could have been sold for the benefit of the poor. Did that impulsive action of hers cause his displeasure? Why else would he have suggested that they should stop attending fellowship that same day? They had not been in fellowship now for over fourteen months and could no longer use the twins as an excuse. What about Levi? He was also missing out and very far from happy. He could not understand why his family were no longer attending fellowship even though his brothers were now surely old enough. Eliana knew Levi had seen babies as young as one month old attend, and they were not the only family who had twins. Levi had recently angrily pointed out to her that Amina and Nebo's family had twins – yet they never even stopped attending!

Eliana knew she often struggled with self-doubt and was not happy. She felt ostracised from her father and his family and now her own husband. It was time to visit Mother Mary again, but how could she, being tied down with two babies? She and Lucas needed to have a serious heart to heart talk. She was not confident to broach the topic of resuming fellowship or their sexual life. She realised that she was afraid to. Was Lucas becoming a stranger?

Then she remembered what Lord Jesus had said. How easy it was to forget, being away from the Centre for over a year! She remembered the messages of hope: *anything is possible to him who believes; bring your needs to God and He will change your attitudes.*

And, from a tune that was sung every day:

'Worthy is the lamb;
Hosanna to the Lamb of God.
He has conquered death,
He has taken all our pain;
He has delivered us from all evil.
We are the new creatures of the Lamb of God;
we shall sing a new song.
We will never look back at the past.
We are marching forward every day in victory
as the new creatures of the Lamb of God.'

True, some brethren did visit occasionally before her family stopped fellowshipping at the Centre. It seemed these brethren were all fooled by the outward appearance of her marriage: a handsome couple in excellent health with the biggest and amazing testimony – their finding each other after ten years! An example of a love story for all other Christians to emulate. There was wealth; there were children, even sons; there was a tremendous abundance of the love of God…

Thinking of God took her mind back to His love. She began to recall in vivid memory all the testimonies she had heard from disciples of Jesus and other brethren at the Centre about the

Lord's Supper. The things He had said about His death. He had predicted His death the evening of a farewell feast with His disciples, but they had not known it was his last. They had assumed they were just celebrating the Passover feast, as God had commanded Moses.

Her mind flashed back to one vivid scene she had been blessed to witness, which came to her whenever she felt low: the picture of Lord Jesus Christ dead on the cross. There had been bad weather. Lord Jesus had been captured at the garden of Gethsemane and taken captive. It was Simeon the Senior who came to give them the news at her home. He was frantically looking for his son, Simeon the Junior, who had fled from the boating shop.

'Eliana, where is your husband, where is my son? Have you seen them?'

'No! What is wrong?'

'They have crucified Lord Jesus at Golgotha. All His disciples, most believers and even His friends are in hiding. Those that did not go into hiding are denying Him openly. Where is Lucas? He and Simeon are not in their shop!'

She remembered how worried he had looked; even fearful. *'No, you can't mean that!'* she had said, shocked. *'Who told you this? Did you see Him on the cross? No, Father Simeon.* Crucified? *What did He do?'* She shook her head and cried tears she didn't know were there.

Simeon eventually recovered from his stupor and comforted her for a while. Then he said, *'Now you understand why I am worried about your husband and my son. The Roman soldiers are seizing anyone who is a follower or a believer in the new faith!'*

'Don't worry, Father Simeon,' she had managed when she felt a bit calmer. *'Your son and probably Lucas too are likely to blend in as unbelievers.'* She recalled that she had deliberately avoided saying that it was easy for both men to deny Jesus in times of

adversity. They were very new creatures. Simeon the Junior only attended the Centre when there were celebrations of weddings and child dedications.

'Lucas is likely to have taken Simeon the Junior with him,' she had said after a few moments of silence.

'You'd think so. Just look at the weather. It has turned dark, and the rain has suddenly become like a storm.'

She stood up. 'I'm going to Golgotha now. I must see Lord Jesus. I'm sure my family is there. I didn't feel too well this morning, but now I feel energised to go.'

Simeon shook his head. 'You must be out of your mind. Did you not hear all I have been telling you about His followers and the soldiers?'

Eliana loosened her hair and unveiled her head. She would become the 'Miriam' personality so that the enemies of the Lord would be fooled. They would see her as a 'sinner' and let her be. Putting on her thickest cloak, she set off to Golgotha, huddling down against the storm. She recalled her mother saying she would never forget the storm that took place soon after the miracle of Lord Jesus feeding the five thousand. That had been a miracle storm, bringing healing to many people. Now she sensed that many people were going to be healed under this afternoon storm, and she was glad of it. The rain would wash out her hair and all the filth it had represented when she was a prostitute. Even as she stepped out into the deluge, with Simeon looking at her with mixed feelings of shame and pride, she knew that she would not cut off her hair as she had purposed. It was part of her testimony and her new identity.

She had seen Him. He had not been recognisable. Who was that bunched up creature on that cross, leaking out a mixture of blood and oil and water? From head to toe, He was bleeding. His flesh was torn. It was a wonder He had not died from the beating. There had been no crowd. Just the soldiers guarding Him, who had surprisingly ignored her. Where was everyone?

As she looked upon the crucified Christ in her memory, her mind and soul connected, and she remembered messages long buried and dormant in her. *There is no shame for those who follow Jesus. No condemnation.* Yes! Why were she and her husband feeling condemned? Suffering needlessly? Surely Lord Jesus's death would be in vain if the believers lived in condemnation and not in freedom? He gave His life for them! The New Creatures were to move forward in life; to enjoy their callings, talents, marriages, and love, and not to put rocks in their paths. They were meant to be enjoying their flourishing faith and the salvation package of the new believer. They were no longer under the laws and traditions of the Rabbis and Elders. They were blessed and not cursed. They were saved. They were new creatures! The righteous of God in Jesus Christ.

She suddenly sensed God's calling on her. *She would open a school for women, including unbelievers, prostitutes, and those who were new creatures, and teach them how to live their lives in fulfilment and peace without condemnation. She would remind them that they were justified by their faith in Lord Jesus and were no longer slaves to their Jewish tradition. 'Daughters of Abraham'. That would be the name of her school! She would teach them that Lord Jesus was the perfect sacrifice for them and everyone. The perfect source for help. They could trust Him with their toughest, deepest, and most impossible problems. Even sex. Nothing was too shameful for our Lord, who had experienced the cruellest, humiliating, most debasing and shameful death; crucified on the cross, naked but for a piece of cloth. He was their perfect friend, and* anything *could be said to Him. He would listen and answer.*

She was so full of testimonies – even ones she had not shared at the Centre.

She suddenly became conscious of a burden and heaviness in her heart. She knew that many new believers were struggling in one way or the other and she was not alone. They all needed to stay firmly in the body of believers, encouraging one another, not bottling up their issues. She turned to Heaven for help, and this time she was able to connect with Abba. Only a week ago she had been unable to pray, but now she finally could...

'Abba, take me and my family back to the Centre to join other believers. I want to go back and be a blessing. I am eager and excited to start the idea of the school You dropped into my spirit this night. Please touch the hearts of my father, my stepbrothers and other believers who are struggling emotionally with the consequences of abiding with the new life You taught us. We are new creatures. This new life is not automatic, Lord. It takes a while for each one of us to adjust. And even Lucas, here. Don't forget him. Touch him. Even now. In the name of Lord Jesus Christ, I have asked. Amen. Thank You, Abba.'

Feeling lighter, calmer and at peace with herself, she recalled someone sharing a great testimony at the Centre. It was about how Lord Jesus had cursed a fig tree and the fig tree had completely died by the following day. He had told His friends that they too could do likewise if they had faith and did not doubt. Lord Jesus had also said one could tell a mountain to go into the sea and it would obey! She couldn't work out why she was remembering all this now, but then it dawned on her that she had more understanding because she had meditated on the cross of Lord Jesus. That was why she could hear His message of faith; that was why she could pray to Abba. She realised that her burden had been lifted off her. She felt free in her very depths. She realised that God had just released her from the oppression of tradition and the Law. Her emotions were opened up, her shame taken away – she was not guilty of her past! She was Eliana, a new creature.

It was time to free Lucas…

It was a chain she had started. Others would catch it in time.

With her mind turned to Lucas, she discerned that he was in a world of doubt, pain, and confusion, and she was not surprised. They had cut themselves off from God by cutting themselves from the assembly of the brethren. They were not focussing on the breadth of God's love, but instead fixating on their problems. Abba was in control. He would not have given them their testimony and their miracle all for nothing. Lord Jesus said all things were possible to those who believed that He was God. She believed Lord Jesus was God and that His plans for her family were for good and not evil. He would turn things round. She was going to believe that God would turn things round this night.

I will start with Dinah. She, too, is now a new creature…

'My lord.' It was a soft whisper, spoken with all her love as she turned to Lucas. She sat up and completely stripped herself of all her clothing. She did not stop to wonder what he might be thinking. She was a new creature. No more condemnation. She let out her hair and cupped her husband's face as she asked him how he would like to have her.

Lucas knew what was happening. 'Kneel and turn your back to me.' He removed his loin cloth, and he was soon transported to the world he had prayed for. God had answered an unspoken prayer and a desire of his heart. This was another testimony, but he knew he would never say it at the Centre. Nevertheless, he and his family would resume going to the Centre this Friday. If people asked questions, he would leave it to his dear 'Dinah' to answer them.

No, *Eliana*. That was who she was. She was gifted in that way, he realised.

CHAPTER 3

You must be born again.
John 3:3

Therefore, since we are surrounded by such a great cloud of witnesses,
let us throw off everything that hinders and the sin that so easily entangles,
and let us run with perseverance the race marked out for us.
Hebrews 12:1

Lucas felt so spiritually lifted at the Centre, and his soul praised God. *Why did I stop coming to the Centre? Oh, my Lord, forgive me for ever doubting or being ashamed of the blessings You have blessed me with. Forgive me for preventing my family going to a place they could continue to grow in Your wisdom and be encouraged. How did I ever let that happen?* He focussed his attention back on the speaker, who was giving a testimony of how he had been radically changed. Lucas did not know him. There were so many new faces...

'He bore our sickness, sins, fears and failures on that cross,' the speaker was saying. 'We are new creatures! Hallelujah! Of course, the devil is jealous of ME and YOU. He tried several times to plant confusion in my life and family. Can you imagine? I was listening to my mind, where the devil was waiting for me. He reminded me of how I used to be evil; destroying people's lives as I stole young innocent children and turned them into sex slaves. I betrayed people's trust with all manner of false claims, deceiving them about the safety of their children. The devil reminded me of my past and lured me away from the peace of a new creature in Jesus Christ. I became tormented, plagued with self-hatred and loathing. I realised the importance of developing discernment in our spirits, because the devil is the enemy of the new creature. Now... enough of my testimony. I am so excited! *Praise the Lord, Brethren!*'

'Praise the Lord,' the assembly excitedly chorused.

'Who else has a testimony?'

'Meee!' piped up an excited eleven-year-old.

Two people were very surprised at this, for different reasons. It was not common for children to give their testimonies. For Lucas, this boy was his son, Levi! He had not been the perfect father and had recently made up his mind to change his attitude to this boy who had accepted him as father after their reconciliation. How could he explain to the boy that he had doubted he was really his father and sent him away at the age of two? What was Levi going to say? Had he understood the testimonies concerning the reconciliation between his parents and how he fitted in their miracle? Lucas suddenly felt anxious. This eleven-year-old he still saw as a small child was very much grown up. Could Levi have noticed his father's fondness and even partiality for his twin brothers?

Eliana was very surprised too, but for a different reason: she could imagine what her son might say. How many times had he begged to be allowed to continue attending the Centre? But she was surprised at his boldness. She knew he could be outspoken, but she also knew he feared Lucas, even after so wanting a father. He was jealous, too; he had on several occasions been severely reprimanded because the way he showed his jealousy of the twins.

But now she saw and understood things clearly. Levi was not jealous. He had very badly missed coming to the Centre AND he feared his father. She had been so preoccupied with the twins and with improving her relationship with Lucas, she had not given Levi due attention, and she felt very guilty. When had she last told him testimonies of Lord Jesus? Before she had reconciled with Lucas, when he was living with her mother and thought she was his sister? Who did he keep company with these days? *Am I a good mother to a growing up child?* There she was, thinking of running a school! Was she supposed to tell him of her past? Certainly not! That was not for children. He had no business with that aspect of her life. She hoped his grandmother had had the wisdom to give him a reasonable explanation for why she had brought him up while his father looked for his mother. How did Rachel explain to him why his mother was absent? She wasn't sure, but it seemed that whatever Rachel had told him seemed to suffice. She kept it at the back of her mind that she would ask her mother about it. Time had flown so fast…

Now, she kept her attention on the last speaker as he left the platform. She was shocked when she recognised the man who had just given his testimony. He was Kabul, the man who had abused her many years ago! How had recognition failed her at first and all the while he gave his testimony? She had realised he was a believer when he gave her back her wages in Capernaum. What was he doing in Jerusalem? She would find out later. Levi was speaking.

'Praise the Lord, brethren!' The hall became hushed instantly, his listeners wearing looks of encouragement. 'A miracle has happened! Three months ago, I was so, so unhappy. I told my mother I wanted to start attending the Centre again, and she said I should talk to Jesus about it. I cried and begged her.' He paused. 'I left her and went to ask my father. I was so scared, but I still went and asked if we could start coming to the Centre again. He did not ask why I had been crying. He just said I should get the answer from my mother. I went to my room and told Jesus that if He allowed us to come back here, I will give a testimony! Praise the Lord, brethren!'

'Praise the Lord!' everyone in the room shouted, clapping their hands.

After the fellowship, there was a call out for those who wanted to come into the new faith. To Eliana's surprise and, she was sure, her husband's too – and indeed all who were watching – she saw Nicodemus, a strong member of the Jewish elders' council and a teacher of the law. Everyone saw him come forward. Who else had come to faith while they had not been attending? Those who were saved today would give their testimony the next Friday. Her husband tugged her arm, and she realised that she had been lost in thought. She saw what her husband was drawing her attention to: a lot of people who were not of the new faith had been encouraged to come forward by the courage of Nicodemus. Her heart swelled as she saw her father, Asher, and her stepbrother Dan amongst the cluster of people who were coming forward. She was riveted, looking through the crowd for more people she could identify. All through this, believers were excitedly clapping their support to the people who wanted to become new creatures.

Eliana clapped frantically, and she did not try to stop the tears that flowed from her eyes. When had she last cried like this? She was sobbing aloud, but so were many others. It was a miracle happening before their very eyes. Eliana knew her mother was somewhere in the room, but she could not see her. She was usually careful not to look around when in the fellowship; Lucas might think she was looking out for Josef. She had discerned that he was still very jealous of Josef, and both men seemed to keep away from each other.

The Rabbi blew the shofar to turn people's attention back to fellowship. It was time for prayer: to lead the new creatures at the front to God. 'Repeat after me,' Apostle Mark began solemnly. *'God, we thank You that You sent Jesus to be the Truth, Light and Way. Thank you for Gethsemane. Thank You for Calvary. Thank You for the Cross. For these New Creatures here, please give them Your hope and strength, that they will all see things Your way and never look back. Strengthen them physically and spiritually to pray always, and give them the passion to remain steadfast. We pray that Your Spirit will continue to stir all Jews who are struggling to become New Creatures.* God bless you all,' he said to finish. 'Please be bold by the power of the Holy Spirit to give your testimony next Friday. This will encourage and bless others. Go in peace.' He looked out at the crowd. 'Now. Next, can we have people who have backslidden in their hearts, through doubt?'

Levi expected that there would be the usual fellowship of people after the session was over: families and friends hugging each other and catching up. He saw that his parents were surrounded by the usual crowd of people fawning over his twin brothers. Nobody would fawn over him, anyway. He saw his opportunity and slipped off gladly. He remembered how Lord Jesus, as a boy, had also slipped away from the gathering of his family and was found at the temple. What had made young Jesus slide away? Of course, he could guess. He was ignored by the adults, as usual. He was that son whose birth had evoked questions that no one wanted to answer, discuss or explain…

Levi looked for his grandmother. He saw a few people he recognised, who he knew recognised him too. He tried to greet them, but they pretended not to see him. No one seemed interested in him anymore; the miracle boy had become old and stale news following all those months of his family's absence. He saw Mother Tamar. He saw Father Josef. He knew his mother had always liked him, and he liked him too, so he stopped to greet him. Father Josef did not take his eyes away or pretend not to see him.

'Look! He even remembers my name. Our good Ariel… I mean, oops, it is Levi now. My, my, my! You have grown so tall already.' Levi was clasped in a loving embrace. 'That was a brilliant testimony, Levi. I am so proud of you. That kind of boldness and determination will make you a leader one day. Keep it up, son.'

Savouring the embrace and praise of this tall, handsome man, who was his secret role model, Levi heard Josef's wife speak, and the magic of the moment was broken; probably gone forever.

'Oh, whose son is this?' she asked for conversation's sake but with a genuine smile. She was not going to store the information in her head. She would ask the same question when she next saw him.

Josef smiled. 'Of course, you know Lev—'

His wife cut him short. 'Oh, yes, the miracle son of Eliana! How could I not recognise you? Forgive me! Where are your parents?'

Levi pointed shyly behind Josef. Josef did not look back, but his wife did, and before she could say anything, Father Josef spoke. 'Alright, son. Send our greetings to your parents. I know you remember us.'

Clever man. Levi nodded his head.

'Your parents know where you are in this crowd?'

Question for question's sake?

'Don't get lost, son. You wouldn't want another miracle!'

Expensive joke, but very funny. Levi laughed as he moved away, knowing he was always shy in this man's presence. He would never forget the great disappointment he had felt that day many months ago when he realised Josef was not going to be his new father.

He continued to wade through the crowd. There was no need for him to keep his eyes down. No one would remember the miracle boy. He had grown much taller, like many boys his age. Where was Grandma Rachel? He had to get to her before she found his parents or before she left.

Someone else saw him and shouted in the din. 'Arieeel!'

'Timmm!'

The adults were shoved out of the way as both boys collided into each other's embrace. Levi saw that Aunty Adah, Timothy's mother, had joined them and was affected by their emotions. Levi preferred the shortened form of Timothy's name. Capernaum life with Tim seemed a world and a lifetime away, but it all came back vividly to Levi now: their brotherhood; the early dawn of house chores done together; school days and lessons in the Torah; the nights they shared sleeping alternately together in his home or Timothy's; the competitions of earnings; their dreams of both wanting a father; their eavesdropping at adult conversations… and, oh, the list was endless. Levi was not surprised that they both cried to see each other.

The same thoughts that had flashed through Levi's mind in half a second had flashed through Timothy's as well. They continued to call each other's name repeatedly; no other conversation seemed possible. How Tim loved the name Ariel. It suddenly occurred to him that Levi was given different names by different people. His grandma and Timothy's family still called him Ariel. Levi's mother used to call him Adam, but Levi's father and the rest of the world called him Levi so Eliana did too, when she remembered to. Tim preferred Ariel, though, and had missed his friendship and brotherhood, especially the closeness they had shared in the past. Tim recalled the secret Levi's grandma,

Mother Rachel, had told Levi about Eliana when she went to Jerusalem to prepare a new home for them. She had been gone for a week. That was when Eliana was Levi's 'sister'. It seemed ages ago.

Since Eliana had joined Levi and Mother Rachel, time had moved so fast; even faster since he had been reconciled with his new parents. He knew his father had last seen him when he was just two years old. Mother Rachel, who had been his 'mother', became his grandmother while Eliana, his 'sister', became his mother. Levi saw himself like a boat tossed about on the stormy waves of an angry Galilean sea; lost in the strong currents and diverted from its course. His relationship with the only mother and brother he had known for ten years was suddenly gone.

He responded to Timothy and Aunty Adah's questions, but they would be amazed if they knew what was going through his mind at the same time.

'Where is Ariel?' Mother Rachel asked. Her eyes were still red from the reunion with her daughter and family. They had shared so many testimonies. The room was getting less rowdy as many people had left the Centre to go home.

'Ariel? You mean *Levi*.' Lucas hoped that from the way he had spoken, Mother Rachel would know that he did not approve of his son being called Ariel. 'Levi must have sneaked off to be with his own friends,' he explained.

'I hurried here to see you all. Levi must have rushed off to where I usually sit. Let me go back and—'

'No, wait, Mother Rachel. When he can't find you, he would come back here,' Lucas advised. *What is wrong with the rascal? He needs discipline, and he will get it.* He would scold him as soon as he found him. His mother was spoiling him so much, probably to make up for the lost years. Why would he rush off without permission?

And then, sure enough, there he was, approaching them with an excited smile on his face, his eyes pinned only on his grandma. Lucas raised his right hand to halt Mother Rachel, who he saw was about to fawn over the lad. 'There you go, you rascal!' he bellowed angrily. 'How dare you take off without letting your parents know? You did not even think of how you might help with your brothers. If this repeats itself, you will be denied favours and privileges as well as being severely punished. Apologise at once!'

'I am so sorry.' Levi's voice quivered through lips trembling with emotion, his eyes swimming with tears. He saw his mother and grandma share a look of surprise in their swiftly shared glance. His grandmother shook her head, sadness and pain in her eyes. As young as Levi was, he understood that she did not want to interfere. That would be undermining Lucas's authority as a family head. She was only a woman.

His mother, however, was bolder. 'My lord,' she said, 'please do not be offended. It is just like twelve-year-old Jesus, when he strolled off from his family after the meeting. Levi is just a boy too.'

'No, Eliana! He is a child who has a father. Not a spoilt lad brought up by people who do not care what child discipline is about.'

Lucas dragged his family out of the Centre in haste, fuming. Over what? Levi didn't know. His father carried Logan while his mother carried Luke, the younger twin.

At least he himself now had some respite from carrying a baby all day.

As he wiped his eyes, he knew that there was no way of asking his grandmother if he could spend a day with her. What was he thinking? Who would help his mother take care of the twins? Why did God give him twin brothers? Initially, he had been excited before they were born. He had not minded the idea of having a sibling, like some other children his age had, but they were too young for him. Was this going to be the story of his life – a carer for the twins and other siblings to come? His mother now schooled him at home, so he could help out with the twins. *What about him?* Who was his caretaker? His father went to work all day. His mother was drawn apart in her attention to the family, house chores and going to the shop while he minded the twins. How long ago did he overhear his parents talking about another baby they were expecting soon? Maybe, if it was a boy, he would be named Lazarus or Laban or Lemuel.

Just as they stepped out of the Centre, a wild thought came into his mind. *What if Mother has another set of twins?* He let out a loud sob in anguish.

And there, in front of everyone, his father slapped him hard. 'I cannot tolerate a big boy like you sobbing like an infant,' he yelled. 'Hold it in, this instant!'

Eliana pleaded with his father, holding his arm. Maybe she was embarrassed that Father Josef and other friends were watching or listening. But his father continued. 'What are you teaching Logan and Luke?'

To everyone's utmost shock, Levi broke away and ran into the Centre, just as Luke started to whimper. He heard his mother call him. *'Adammmm!'* His main intent was to go out through the North Exit and stay away for as many days as it would take for his family to find him. He hoped he could catch up with his grandmother, but if he failed to, he knew whose house he would go to. One thing he knew with certainty was that his father would not chase after him.

He was right.

He swore within himself that he would never return until all the mysteries of the 'miracles' concerning his life in connection to his father, his mother and his grandmother were all plainly explained to him. As far as he was concerned, Lucas and Eliana were strangers in the guise of adopted parents.

Eliana had never been in such a fix. She had just seen Levi exhibit behaviour she would never have imagined, and she was being blamed. Her own Adam! What was happening? Even after she called after him, he did not come back.

Lucas did not make any attempt to go after him. 'This is all your fault! What do you teach him each day when I am at work?'

She ignored the accusation. 'Please go after him quickly. Please hurry up, my lord.'

'No, I won't,' he said.

Eliana tried to hand Luke over to him.

He shook his head. 'You won't, either. He knows where he is going. I saw him being embraced by Josef. He knows their house. If he doesn't catch up with them, he might stay with his grandmother. Can we go home? It's not fair on the twins. They need their bed very soon.' He heaved Logan to his shoulder. 'Carry Luke. Come on.'

'How will I be able to sleep, not knowing where my son is?'

Her husband walked away without answering.

To her relief, Sister Elizabeth came forward with Micah, her husband. Their children were much older and had gone home. 'Do you need help with the baby? You must be tired, seeing you are carrying another one within you.' She smiled as she bent to carry baby Luke.

'My God,' Eliana thought, *'how would she know? I am not even showing in any way!'*

'Where is your older son? He usually helps out. I thought I saw him with you all this evening.'

'Yes. He has gone to stay with his grandmother. I am only worried whether he would remember the way to her house. He has never gone on his own.'

'We could help,' Micah offered. 'Where does Mother Rachel now live?'

'Please be quick,' Eliana said, beginning to cry. 'At the second house entering Kiv. It is where my father, Asher, lives. You cannot miss it. There is a big goat pen in front.'

She felt some relief as Father Micah went straight after Levi, while Mother Elizabeth carried the child.

'It was wonderful seeing your father come out to the front.' Elizabeth sounded excited.

'Yes! Though he did not come to meet me. My mother thinks he was shy. She too was surprised to see him here today, because they did not come together. My mother didn't know we were at the centre, either, but Levi's testimony let her know we were around. My father left immediately.'

'Still, how come Levi did not follow Grandma Rachel home?' Elizabeth asked.

'He did not make up his mind on time. It was just at the spur of the moment.'

'He might have caught up with her, you know.'

'That is my prayer.'

'It is well. You shouldn't worry. He is a big boy.' A pause. 'Ahh, look at your babies! They are so well behaved. How old are they now?'

'Eighteen months, now.' *I feel emotionally spent and exhausted, Lord. Why?*

'Oh, good. They will be at least two years old when your next baby arrives.'

Silence.

'You must be wondering how I know.'

Eliana nodded, but her gaze was far away with her husband, who was walking so fast it was as if he was trying to ensure they never caught up with him. What was it like to live with Lucas when he was angry? She wasn't quite sure. Dinah had been a simple, obedient housewife. Entirely submissive in every way, she lived by works to achieve perfection with all her strength, soul, and body. Lucas had never been angry with her Dinah personality all through the two years she had lived with him.

Not until the day they celebrated Levi's second birthday…

Lucas did not realise how fast he was walking, but he was conscious of his thoughts boiling over and spilling out to his mood. It hurt him that the peace, inner joy and inexplicable contentment and harmony he had enjoyed while at the Centre had been replaced with anger directed at his family and self-remonstration. He knew he was angry and jealous about Levi showing so much love to Josef. He was sure the boy had gone seeking Josef; he had fallen so naturally into the other man's arms and did not seem to be in a hurry to do anything else. Was his coming to the Centre going to be a constant reminder of 'Jocheb and Miriam'? Jocheb had been transformed to Josef, the new creature, and Miriam to Eliana. But they had been lovers, and Jocheb had badly wanted to marry Miriam. *'You are very timely, Lucas,'* she had said. *'Josef would have beaten you to it, a day more!'*

There were brethren who, in their excitement at giving testimonies, said too much. There was no need for them to mention certain details that had occurred between Josef and Eliana in the past. How did they expect him to feel? Mother Ahuva told him how Josef had been willing to follow Miriam to look for her son and how he had pursued her for three years! She had also told him how Jocheb had revealed his true identity to Miriam. *'God is wonderful,'* Mother Ahuva had said, *'shielding and protecting Eliana's heart from falling to Josef because Abba had a plan for Eliana with you, Lucas.'*

The damage had already been done. This was why he had stopped his family attending fellowship all those months and discouraging brethren to visit. He and his wife needed breathing space to heal and build bridges for the ten years they had been apart.

He knew he was a very private person and did not relish his private life spat out in the open. He knew that most people were disappointed that he did not testify how he had coped without his wife in ten years and about the day he found out about her.

He liked Mother Rachel. She was sensible. She did not go about telling everyone how God had led her to find him. She too had a painful past which she did not share all the time. Testimonies were meant to edify God, not to be used as a tool to encourage household gossip.

He was not happy that seeing Josef had sparked up his jealousy, or that he had vented his anger on Levi and on his wife. If he had seen Levi with Josef, then Eliana too must have seen them together. When he had asked after Levi before Rachel came to them, she had pretended ignorance. Why did Eliana still feel uneasy where Josef was concerned? He found himself falling back into the predicament at his office with Simeon the Junior almost a week ago. Should they leave Jerusalem? If they left Jerusalem and moved to another town, would he meet a former client of Eliana?

Soon he arrived home. He was angry and guilty at the same time, but it was all her fault. She was not firm enough with Levi. Without even looking backwards, he let himself into their house.

CHAPTER 4

This is how we know that we live in Him and He in us.
He has given us His Spirit.
We have seen and testify that the father has sent His Son
to be the Saviour of the world.
If anyone acknowledges that Jesus is the Son of God,
God lives in them and them in God.
And so we know and rely on the love God has for us.
1 John 4:13-16

'How did you enjoy fellowship at the Centre today?'

It was time to offer an olive branch. Supper was done with, and the twins were in bed. Eliana's routine had seemed the same, even though Levi wasn't around. She had tidied up, prepared their supper, and served Lucas. She had taken her bath and had come down to keep him company. Levi would have gone off to his room if he had been in; he didn't seem to enjoy adult company these days.

Suddenly she realised how, as parents, they were centring their lives around work and the twins. They had been neglecting their eldest son.

Lucas did not answer her immediately. She discerned that he was feigning being too wrapped up in thought to have heard her.

She reframed her question. 'It was wonderful fellowship at the Centre today, wasn't it?'

'Please ask or say something else. The answer to your question was already confirmed when we were greeting brethren. Surely, you must have heard me say to Elder Simeon how great I felt.'

Eliana felt that even after almost two years it was still difficult to transform from Dinah the stooge-wife – docile and ever wanting to please at any cost – to Eliana the independent wife; strong, wilful, and very enterprising. His reply threw her off guard completely, and she did not know which of her personalities to switch to. Dinah took complete control of their sexual life. Right now, though, she decided to serve him with the bold, unflinching, and cold personality of Safirah, and the next question she asked threw him off his feet. 'My lord, do you still doubt that Levi is yours?'

They looked at each other in silence. He wondered where she found the audacity and courage to ask him such an impertinent question. Levi must have inherited this streak of forwardness from his mother. No orthodox Jewish woman dared ever raise a question like that and then continue to stare at her husband unabashed, as if to deliberately wage a silent battle of wills. His authority was at stake. Whichever way he answered, he was paving the way for more of such disrespect. She deserved a slap. When he realised she was not going to lower her gaze, he considered it a fight against his manhood, so got up almost menacingly then stood over her. 'If you do not want me to believe you are indeed a New Creature, washed spotlessly clean of all your past sins, your filthy life and your old faith, repeat what you just asked, Eliana.'

She pulled back the Safirah spirit. She had to be wise. At least he now knew that she was not all weak. She thought for a moment, then offered him the Reubena personality as a compromise. Lowering her eyes, she got on her knees and meekly apologised.

In the interval of that silence, while Lucas decided if this was the right moment to lay plain what was on his mind on the table of their hearts, they were both startled at the sudden light tap on their door. Lucas assumed Levi had been brought back home, and despaired as he saw his wife perk up at the same thought and rise from her knees.

Opening the door, he met both Elder Benjamin, who lived in Kiv, and Father Micah; both members of the Intervention Team. There was no Levi, but they did not look like harbingers of bad news.

'Shalom,' the men greeted.

He stared at them in surprise. 'Shalom,' he said after a moment's pause. He gestured for them to enter, but they stayed their ground.

'Levi is in good hands,' Elder Benjamin said, a broad smile lighting his face as he saw Eliana joining her husband at the door. 'Abba is aware of the situation in this home and has permitted it. It is His wish that you both have your privacy and the opportunity for restitution, and time to examine your marriage truthfully. Peace only comes when couples submit everything. No secrets.'

'This is it. No secrets. This is the time. I thought I had escaped it. Abba God, there are indeed no secrets hidden from You. I will experience what Josef felt when he opened up his past to me when I was Miriam and he was Jocheb. God, help me tonight!' Eliana prayed her thoughts.

'After your time together, go and pick up Levi from Mother Adah and Timothy.'

As they turned their backs to go, Eliana quickly spoke. 'Please come in and have tea. Do not refuse, as we shall take it that you shake your feet against our home. We receive your message in peace.'

Lucas looked at his wife. This was not Dinah, neither was it the one who had been insolent some minutes ago. He wondered, for the first time since they were married, how many other personalities she possessed which were still alien to him.

'Thank you, Father Lucas and Mother Eliana,' both men replied together as they entered the couple's majestic abode. It was Father Micah's first time in this home, and he was flabbergasted. He had heard how wealthy Eliana had become from several years of investing in the business of prostitution. She had accumulated property and land in Jerusalem and Judea. The rugs, the chandeliers, the silver, the gold plaited pottery. The water cistern at the back of the room, where people could wash their feet and faces, provided hot and cold water! She could have been living in Egypt or Rome. Indeed, this was the woman who had lavished a perfume worth a year's wages on Lord Jesus's feet! He was so mesmerised that when his name was called, he was startled.

'Father Micah... Father Micah! What wisdom has God laid on your heart to share with our brethren here?'

He had been listening with one ear to Elder Benjamin giving his usual opening talk about Abraham and Lot who could not dwell together because of the strife between their families and their business associates. It was wisdom that they separated. For couples, it was not wisdom, as they were one; joined together by God. Separation would only lead to spiritual death. The devil tried to separate couples by using the blessings God gave them such as their children, their strengths, their health, or their wealth. It was therefore up to couples to be discerning and remember that it was the devil who was the enemy, not one another.

All of this talk passed vaguely through Father Micah's memory as he said, 'Thank you very much, Elder Benjamin. Dear brethren, even if we have all these blessings from God, we may still not have peace if we don't keep our faith in Lord Jesus Christ. Because the spirits of anxiety, low self-esteem, fear, worry, anger, dissatisfaction, and many other negative spirits would attack.'

Elder Benjamin knew what was coming next as he listened to the usual advice Father Micah gave to couples who needed spiritual intervention in their marriage.

'What we all need is the peace of God which Lord Jesus said He left with each of us, not the worldly type of peace.' He paused and looked at each of them, as if expecting some comment. 'This means no stress, no conflict; just wholeness and self-confidence. This is what Shalom means. Listen, my brethren, my cousin Apostle Thomas told of a time when Lord Jesus commanded a dangerous and threatening storm to stop. The sea and the winds immediately obeyed and became very calm. It was a miracle! Why do I refer to this incident? I will tell you.' He looked at Elder Benjamin as if to get his approval to enjoy the luxury of time. Elder Benjamin sanctioned with a nod.

'Whatever storm you are facing in your marriage or family, you can both call upon Lord Jesus to speak to that storm through His Holy Spirit living in you. Say it out – *peace be still. Peace be still.*'

He let silence fall for a moment.

'Storms come into our lives, and the prayer is: *Lord Jesus, don't you care if we drown?* That is what His disciples asked Him in the boat. Guess what? As soon as He was awake, he asked what they were afraid of! So, my dear Lucas and Eliana, we can learn from that experience that whatever our fears, only Lord Jesus Christ can help. In fact, Lord Jesus asked them if they still had no faith after witnessing all His miracles. That question applies to you both too. After all the miracles and blessings God has given you both to experience within the space of under two years, are you still not able to trust God? I will stop here, so that Elder Benjamin can pray for you.'

Father Benjamin bowed his head. *'Sovereign God, we thank You for ruling and reigning in our lives no matter what goes on. Still the storm and the hearts of Lucas, Eliana, Levi, and every other member of their family, in Jesus Christ's name, we ask, Amen.'*

'Amen.'

Abba's angels were on standby, and in less than a second the prayerful desires, wishes and requests had been carried straight to Abba's ears. Abba gave His approval. The prayers were in line with His purpose. Another set of His ministering angels who delivered answers to prayers as fast as light were sent out, and they deposited Abba's will in the hearts of: Lucas; his wife Eliana; Levi their first son; Asher, Eliana's father; Rachel, Eliana's mother; Dan, Asher's first son; Keziah, Dan's wife; Tobiah, Asher's second son; Biliah, Tobiah's wife; Rebecca, Lucas's sister; and Amaziah Abraham, Rebecca's husband.

Levi felt relieved after Father Benjamin and Father Micah had left. It had been a long day. He reviewed the events of the evening as he lay down in bed, waiting for sleep. He remembered the tension he had felt before finding Aunty Adah and Timothy and wondering what their reaction would be to see him following them home. He never caught up with them. He remembered his frustration as he waited around the street by their home, trying not to bring undue attention to himself. He had also been concerned that his father might change his mind and come after him, but he did not. He had made up his mind that he would very meekly beg to spend the night with Timothy.

He had tried not to look anxious as time went on and it was getting darker, people disappearing into their homes. At last, someone had noticed him and interrogated him. He was duly informed that Timothy and his mother were dining three houses away. Relieved, he knocked timidly at the door of that home.

Timothy shouted his name as he opened the door but immediately knew something was wrong. 'Ariel! Mama, it is Ariel, and his eyes have blood.' Levi had broken down and wept as the scene before his flight flashed through his mind.

Timothy held him as his mother gave an apology to their hosts. 'It was very kind of you to have invited us for dinner, Father Jonah. We will stay longer next time. Please allow me to go and see to my son here. He looks in bad shape.'

Before Levi knew it, they were back at Tim's house, where they fawned over him and cared for him. *This was more like it.* When he had finished his supper and recounted his tale of the evening, he began to settle down. He wondered about how his mother was coping without his help as Timothy brought him up to date about his own life. In the middle of this paradise, Father Benjamin and Father Micah knocked on the door and were ushered in by Aunty Adah. Levi knew instantly why they were here. They explained that they had first gone to Mother Rachel's house, and she had directed them here. Mother Rachel had been busy bathing her new step granddaughter, Batia, and had sent word that she would see Ariel later.

Aunty Adah had taken the two fathers outside. On cue, Levi and Tim had at the same time jumped up quietly and gone over to the door to eavesdrop, a big grin plastered on their faces. They winked at each other as they listened to the entire conversation between the adults. They left the door just at the right time and continued as if they had been catching up on each other.

Aunty Adah came in. 'I told them that you are fine. I have been told to tell you that you can remain here for now.'

'Really?' he had asked, feigning excitement.

'Yes. Stay with us until you are picked up by your father.'

'He won't come. I will have to go on my own.'

'No. Father Benjamin insisted you remain with us until you are fetched.'

Even now, lying in the darkness beside his friend and brother, he processed the news with mixed feelings. His mother would need his help when his father went to work. There were times he stayed with the twins while she went to bathe, toilet or do some kitchen work. He wondered again how she would cope if he continued to wait here till he was fetched by his father. He might drop by on his way from work.

He looked at Timothy, who was snoring softly. He had always been an easy sleeper, unlike him. Tim too had grown very tall. Much taller than him! He would grow as tall as Father Josef. Father Josef! He really liked the man. He wondered why he and Mother Razi had no babies, considering they were married about the same time as his new parents.

Apart from Father Josef, only Aunty Adah and Timothy had praised him for his testimony. His mother had smiled proudly, but his father's face had been inscrutable. What had his father thought?

Well, it had been so wonderful going to the Centre. *Thank you, Lord Jesus.* It was great seeing Tim again. Who would have ever believed that he would be spending the night with Tim like old times, talking themselves out till they dozed off! He could feel his eyelids becoming heavy, and he was beginning to feel drowsy. But he did not fall asleep without reflecting on what Tim had said to him: *'Ariel, don't rush your parents to tell you the facts of their past without talking to Lord Jesus first. Remember what He said?'*

When he had raised his eyebrows in a question, Tim had continued. *'Ah, I forgot you have not been for a long time. Lord Jesus said we believers of the new faith should ask anything in His name, and He will do it for us! How about that, Ariel? Try it!'*

He tried it now.

'My God, I ask for my new parents to tell me about how we all got separated in the past. Do not let my father be angry with me for coming here. And please give Father Josef a son, or two if he wants. I cannot think of anything else, but You know everything. Remember, God, I have asked all these things in Jesus Christ's name. Amen.'

He slept instantly and, just then, angels were dispatched by Abba to grant his wishes.

CHAPTER 5

Without Me, you can do nothing.
John 15:5

I will never leave you or forsake you.
Hebrews 13:5

The truth shall set you free. Eliana found this to be so, so true as she thought about the amazing events of the long evening she and Lucas had just experienced after the two church Elders had left them. The unbelievable incidents kept her soul, body, and mind tingling. Not even because they had just made love in the Dinah fashion; this time it was as if all her personalities were combined in the person of Eliana. Freedom was so sweet. It was nothing like she had ever experienced before. She knew that this day really marked the true beginning of their lives as a married couple. Their lives as New Creatures. Everything was now out in the open *(well, except that little lie she'd once told her husband in connection with Josef).* Surely there would never be any more problems in their lives.

She let her mind rewind back to those beautiful moments.

As soon as Lucas had closed the door after the two brethren left, he came towards her and said, 'Eliana, you asked me how I found the fellowship at the Centre earlier on this evening. I am sorry about the way I answered you.'

'Don't worry, my lord. I understood the perspective from which you answered. I am not angry at all.'

'Thank you. Well, I really enjoyed fellowship and even asked Abba to forgive me for denying us all the blessing of joy in His presence and in the company of other brethren. Apostle Othniel, who gave the message, spoke directly to my soul…' He paused.

She seized the opportunity to say, 'I am glad you enjoyed it, my lord. I saw that you came home most evenings feeling low last week.' She summoned up her courage. 'What was responsible for your foul mood last week?'

He gave a deep sigh, and went to sit beside her. Gone was that former attitude of his which could not tolerate his wife questioning his moods or activities. This was a wonder, he realised, as he unburdened himself about his sour moods of the previous week. 'I discouraged Simeon the Junior from coming to fellowship at the Centre!'

Silence fell, but Eliana waited and did not rush on to ask why.

'I deliberately discouraged him because I did not want him to eventually hear the testimony of our marriage.' He paused, and Eliana remained quiet. 'I tormented myself with imaginary problems of the future such as: who would marry our children? Should we move to another town? Would I meet former clients of yours? Well, all that is over now. The message today spoke directly to my heart.' He broke off, nodding his head. 'I was moved to join the group of brethren who felt they had backslidden in their thoughts. Eliana… forgive me for this angry, doubtful attitude I have recently directed at you.'

'My lord, you should forgive me too. I have not been open with you about the whole of my life and person. I am no longer afraid. I am ready to tell you everything you wish to know.'

'That is very good, Eliana. It has occurred to me that we began our reconciled marriage with a grown child, and we have not had any moments between the two of us alone. It is Abba's wisdom that we did not go chasing after Levi. Where do you want to start?' he asked hopefully.

'From what you do not know; I know you already know about my different personalities.'

'Just in bits from your mother, Mother Abigail, and Mother Ahuva. I should hear it from you directly.'

Eliana realised that she was not scared or ashamed. She wanted to be open as possible. She discerned that Lucas still loved her and cared that their marriage should succeed despite the peculiar circumstances surrounding it. She settled herself and said, 'I will tell you everything. It is a long story, my lord.'

Lucas relaxed back, listening.

Eliana took a deep breath, then found herself starting her life story right from the beginning, just as she had done with Mother Abigail when she was Miriam. 'I was called 'E' as a child in the charity home at Nain. I thought I was an orphan as I never knew how I had lost my family. I used to claim that a fire accident had killed them all. It was not until I was five years old that I realised my name was Eliana. Then I was sold to a glass merchant in Sidon, and I renamed myself as Reubena. There I served food and drinks, danced, massaged clients and obeyed whatever commands I was given that satisfied their curiosity or gave them sexual gratification. About eight years later, when I was thirteen, my life changed. A client, Al Basrah, took me to Samaria and resold me to Gwabar, and I renamed myself as Safirah. I was very angry, embittered and full of hatred because Al Basrah had promised me freedom and protection, but he betrayed me. By the age of seventeen, I had become conscious of my power over men and used it to my advantage. I forced Gwabar to take fifty percent of the profits as opposed to ninety percent. I also began estate management at this age. With the help of Gwabar himself, who was afraid for me to leave his business, I bought a property each in Sidon and Samaria which I let out under the name of Miriam. I never realised the name meant 'rebellion'.'

She swallowed and paused as Lucas poured some water for her.

'Thanks,' she said, and after a few sips she continued, a wistful expression playing on her face. 'As I grew older and wealthier, I realised I wanted more from life: a home and a family of my own. It seemed an impossible dream, but I clung to hope and chased my dream until I felt I could make it happen. Finally, I walked out of Gwabar's life and came to Sidon. I renamed myself Dinah and worked as a house servant to Sosthenes and Keturah, who introduced me to you a year later. You know the rest. I was your wife for two years until my cover was exposed on Levi's second birthday by a former client. I then came over to Jerusalem and renamed myself Miriam. For seven years, I continued to invest in property here in Jerusalem and Bethlehem. I met Josef through his sister, Johanna. I met their mother, Abigail. I met Biliah and Tobiah and Razilla and Amina, all through Johanna. They all became believers of the new faith, and they led me to meet Lord Jesus.

'My life turned around. Lord Jesus gave me a mother who turned out to be my real mother. It was Rachel, my mother, who happened to replace me in Sosthenes' household after I had left you. Keturah had taken up Levi, hoping to find him a good home, then Rachel agreed to adopt him till his father asked for him, and the couple agreed.' She paused as Lucas nodded his head. 'She renamed him Ariel. Later, she moved away from Sidon with Levi to Capernaum because she wanted to be cured of her backache – she'd heard about Jesus, the miracle man, and wanted to meet him. She met a friend, Mother Adah, who had a son the same age as Levi. She never went back to Sidon, because

Timothy and Ariel had become inseparable, and she and Mother Adah were like sisters.'

Eliana took a long drink of water. She was amazed to find herself being so open as she continued, revealing how she had invested in estate property in Jerusalem, Sidon, Samaria, and Bethlehem. She was encouraged because her husband had kept a straight face throughout and never once interrupted her. He was a very good listener; she knew he was *really* listening.

After it all spilled out of her, she fell into a relaxed mood and felt peace pervade her soul. How did she never realise she had been carrying a burden? The weight of all her disguised personalities had been stripped and infused into her present person – Eliana.

Now she waited for her husband to tell her what he did in those ten years they were apart.

He embraced her with shiny, teary eyes. 'Thank you so much, Eliana. It is miraculous, the way Abba has connected us all back together! If I knew this much about your past, I would not have been so jealous of Josef and vented my anger on poor Levi this evening. There is one little gap in your story, though. I do not know if this is deliberate or an oversight...' He paused, and then he was silent.

'Please ask, my lord,' she encouraged. 'I would tell you if it was an oversight or not. What clarification or gap do you seek?'

'Back to ten years ago. You said you left Sidon after me sending you away, and you came to Jerusalem to start your life as Miriam. Did you immediately leave Sidon that night to Jerusalem? I know you left with only the clothes you had on that afternoon?'

After a few seconds of silence, she answered, 'Yes, it was deliberate. I wanted you to ask. If you had not asked, I would have found the right time to tell you.'

'Are you going to tell me?' Lucas asked somewhat apprehensively.

'I went to Rebecca, your sister. I told her everything. She promised to help me. I told her I was with child at the time and that even you did not know—'

'You mean...' her husband interrupted. She had never seen his face wear a graver mask. '...You mean Rebecca knew where you were all that time?' He shook his head in disbelief. 'And... a... a child?'

'Yes, but I told her not to let you know so that I did not get killed. I told her that Levi had been taken away by Keturah and begged her to keep an eye on him for me. She promised. I... I asked her if she would keep the child I was carrying if it lived until such a time that I was ready to be responsible for its upkeep... and she agreed. My lord... we have a ten-year-old daughter. Her name is Leah.'

Lucas was wide-eyed but smiling. 'Why has Abba been so merciful to me? Eliana, I don't know what to say right now. I am so engulfed with all kinds of feelings. Where is Leah now?'

'Still with your sister!'

'I cannot wait to meet her, Eliana. Another testimony for the Centre, next Friday.'

'I know. I assume you want us to go and get her soon.'

'Of course! When did you see her last?'

'The day she was born.'

Her husband stared at her in shock. Then he got up, pulled her arm, and said, 'How about we go up to bed and celebrate our daughter – and your touching, but startling, testimony? I promise to tell you mine after the Sabbath tomorrow.'

'Sabbath? We are new creatures now. I too am very eager to know your story, my lord. What of Levi?'

'What about him?'

'When do we collect him, and how do we explain that he now has a sister? I have never told anyone about Leah.'

'That is why I said we have another testimony to give next Friday. Now, celebration time, Eliana!'

Now, she was still savouring the aftermath of their lovemaking and the way the evening had gone. Feeling very sleepy beside Lucas, who was snoring softly, she realised that if she had insisted on going after her Adam the events of this evening would never have happened.

That same evening, in the household of Josef and Razilla, the incidents at the Centre had ignited a different kind of atmosphere, leading to another engaging dialogue and open confession between man and wife.

Dinner done, with crockery all washed up, Razilla came to join her husband. 'It was exciting seeing Lucas and his family again, Josef. I am happy for them.'

'Yes. The message from Apostle Othniel was so apt. Did you see the way Father Nicodemus stepping out suddenly encouraged many others to be bold and step forward?'

'Yes, I saw Eliana's father and brother also step out. Did you see the way Eliana was crying with joy and clapping in ecstasy?' she asked.

'So did many others.'

'Their son has grown so tall and looks very much like his father.'

'You think so?' he asked.

'Yes.' Some silence. 'What do you think?'

'It is not important. I was expecting you would talk about the message or my proposed trip to Tyre tomorrow.'

Silence, then: 'Josef, I have been thinking.'

'Me too, but you go first.'

'About us.' That jolted him. He assumed she was referring to his continued habit of avoiding the family of Lucas and Eliana. It had made things awkward between him and his wife. He had not gone with her to see their twins when they were born. He deliberately did not go to welcome Lucas and his family back to the Centre and always tried to avoid a chance face-to-face meeting with Lucas or Eliana. Even in conversations, he was evasive. He knew she had noticed the way he skirted around conversations that involved Lucas's household.

About us. What did she have in mind? They had many months ago decided to keep trusting Abba for children and not get stressed or worried. He realised he was anxious. 'Alright.'

'Josef. I have a lot on my mind about us.'

'Razi, you know I will listen. Even if you speak till tomorrow morning, I will be here listening.'

'Both of us will age faster if we do not do something to occupy us while we wait for God's blessings. When you travel on business, I go to work in the bakery and from there, I go to the Centre and return home but still, I am not fulfilled. When you are back home from business, you read until you are tired, but you are not fulfilled. I saw the way you handled Eliana's son. I realised how much you would cherish a child of your own. It might interest you to know that I encouraged Biliah to adopt Abel, their first son, when she became a new creature. She was so full of the love of Jesus and wanted to give love back in her own way. You remember when she and Tobiah gave their testimony of Reuben, their baby son?'

He nodded and said, 'Yes. They both said they thought they were not going to be blessed with children because of their past lives.'

'True. Also, Biliah had contracted a disease which she believed had rendered her barren, and she confided that Tobiah had, too.'

'Really? Tobiah too? I didn't know about that!' Josef suddenly felt uncomfortable as he remembered that Tobiah, like him, was involved with male prostitution. Did Razi suspect that he too had a disease which was preventing their ability to conceive? 'I always thought that their coming together was based on the fact they were outcasts to their very strong Jewish backgrounds.'

'That is true, but he had also contracted this disease that seemed to make him unable to father a child. And then, after adopting Abel, God blessed them with lovely Reuben.'

Again, her husband looked very uncomfortable.

'Josef, do you find it uncomfortable to visit couples who are blessed with newborn infants or children? I don't like going alone all the time, as I have to make excuses for you. I usually visit when you have gone off on business. Can we go together when Eliana has her next baby, please?'

That caught his attention. 'Eliana is pregnant again? Did she tell you this? Because she doesn't look it!'

Razilla nodded. 'It is my prayer that when we both go, we would go with our little one. We could go to the Charity Centre at Nain, and adopt a newborn... please, Josef. God has blessed every one of my friends who were all prostitutes like I was, and I trust He will grant us our own twin sons too like He gave to Eliana.'

'I pray for twin sons too.' He saw his wife become very excited, to the point of tears.

'Josef, please let us go tomorrow... so that by Friday we can present our son as a testimony at the Centre.'

Her husband caught onto the excitement. 'Yes! What shall we call him? Eliphaz? Nathan? What do you have in mind?'

'Abel... or Aaron.'

'Oh, no! Biliah's son is Abel. We will call him Samuel. As the name means 'God has heard', the boy will be anointed and replace our loneliness, our shame, and our sadness at our childlessness as we wait for God to give us more.' Then, holding his wife's hand, he spoke to Abba. *'May Abba do unto us as he did to Tobiah and Biliah, in Jesus Christ's name we pray.'*

'Amen,' they both said together.

'I can't believe how light at heart I now feel, Razi. Why have we been carrying this burden alone and for so long? Come here, my love. Let us go and celebrate the arrival of Samuel. And one more thing, Razi – you are a new creature now. I want you to be free in the love of Lord Jesus Christ. Promise me that as we go and celebrate, you will take off *all* your clothes and *release* the love of your heart and passion, just as you used to for those clients when you were called Eva.'

He saw his wife stiffen.

'How did you know I was called Eva? I never told anyone. I mentioned it to only one person who was far from being a new creature at the time. Tell me.'

Josef folded his arms over his chest. 'So… that same person told me.'

Razi sat in silence for a moment. Then, 'Josef, promise me too that you will stop being uncomfortable around Lucas and Eliana. We have died to ourselves so that Lord Jesus can be glorified. We have sought his Kingdom and righteousness. I have crucified my obsessions and all worldly things. I have put Lord Jesus on my throne, and I am not ashamed to be around others, nor do I feel fear if I see any of my clients because it is Lord Jesus they will see reflected in my life. Josef, I want you to have this attitude: that all who see you are seeing Lord Jesus in a new creature and not the old creature. Please promise me,' she pleaded.

'I promise you, my love.'

'I have always wanted to love you as my heart feels, but I was aware that you were not yet in the Spirit as you were inhibited yourself. This is an answered prayer, Josef. This evening God sent Levi to you, and you embraced him with so much fatherly love that it set me thinking... and it has led to this very fruitful fellowship between us. Oh, Josef, come and shower me with your love. I cannot wait. Tomorrow I will be a mother! Mother Razi!'

'And I am Father Josef,' he murmured softly as he fondly reached for his wife. Laughing like excited children, they went upstairs to their chamber hand in hand, and there, as they made sweet love, the angel heard Abba's command. *Now!*

The angel of Abba dropped the gifts for them.

CHAPTER 6

The righteousness of God in Christ.
Freedom is what we have – Christ has set us free!
Galatians 5:1

The Centre was so crowded this Friday. Levi stretched his neck to see over people, eagerly looking for his parents. He was sure they would come and were seated somewhere. He was determined to beat Tim, who was also searching through the crowd. Because Tim was so tall, he could spot people more easily. He had the added advantage that he was a regular attender, so knew where certain families sat. He had just chirped that he had seen Father Asher and his entire family, then he spotted Josef and Razi, and nudged Levi to look at them. He saw why instantly and stared in surprise: Razi was holding a baby a little younger than his twin brothers. Levi still wanted to be the first to spot his own parents, but he began to wonder about Mother Razi. Who was this baby?

'Look Levi! There's your family, and—'

'Where? Where?'

'Just in front of Father Josef. Can you see the girl sitting in between them? Do you know her?'

'Yes, she was at Father Matthew's party,' Levi lied as he strained to see across the crowd of bobbing heads.

'I don't believe you! Why didn't I see her too?' Tim said.

'Shh,' Tim's mother whispered, her finger pressed to her mouth.

At that point, all the milling brethren settled down as the shofar was brought out. Levi found his mind wandering as the shofar was blown three times, thinking about the tall girl. Who was she? There were many young girls his age and even younger in the Centre, but this girl stood out. Maybe she had joined the church when his family had temporarily stopped coming. Still, why did she sit in between his parents? She had the same long, thick hair as his mother…

Suddenly, he realised why he had not noticed his parents before Timothy did. It was where they sat: they never usually sat anywhere near Father Josef and his family. Levi had looked for them in the opposite direction. They were also in the section for people who had very special and moving testimonies. He frowned, surprised and puzzled, and then he remembered that they had sat in that section when he and his parents were finally and miraculously reunited as a family. *Who was the girl?*

Had his parents even tried to look for him? He'd been away for a week now, and no attempts had been made, although his grandmother had already come to visit him three times. She said she did not want to go to his home until she was certain his father would encourage her to visit. He sighed. What was wrong with all these new creatures? In what way were they new if they were not free to love one another like Lord Jesus did? There was still strife, hurt and pain amongst some of the family members he knew. Take his father's family, for example. His father's sister, Aunt Rebecca, had been completely cut off because her husband was directly related to the family of Judas Iscariot, who were seen as traitors and blamed for Lord Jesus's death. Making the situation even worse was that the main culprit, Judas, had hung himself, thereby soiling every member of his family along with him. Judas Iscariot's family had become like a plague amongst Jews, and no one wanted to be associated with them. Even Levi's grandmother said it was worse than being a leper.

He started as Tim nudged him out of his thoughts, and realised it was the point when everyone had to get up and greet brethren they had not seen since the previous week. But thoughts had cast a dark shadow on his mood, and he refused to get up.

'What's up with you?' Tim said. 'Are you jealous of that girl? Look… your father is coming towards you!'

But Levi thought it was one of the pranks they played on each other and did not budge. He crossed his arms over his body and kept his eyes on his sandals.

'Levi, my beloved son! I have missed you so much. We will catch up on a lot of things.' Lucas bent down and whispered into Levi's ear, 'Please come and join your family. You… you have a new sister, and her name is Leah!'

Levi stared at his father, shocked. Just like that! A new, unknown member of the family had been thrust upon him. It was like before, when he had been unexpectedly reconciled with his parents.

Nothing could really shock him anymore, he realised as he found himself getting up to follow his father. Lucas nodded his head in greeting to Mother Adah, Timothy, and the people around them. Then Levi felt something new as his father put his arm around his shoulders. Something akin to intimacy was transpiring between them, and he could not control the sudden strong emotions that flooded his heart and brought tears to his eyes. He was drowning in a well of mixed emotions: guilt, nostalgia, love, anger, accusation, and a host of complex feelings he could not label and process. He felt horrified that this new sister would always remember her first meeting with him; a red-eyed, sniffing, big baby. He was causing quite a stir. Father Josef and Mother Razi both came towards him with concern, but he was not in the right mood.

His father took him outside and they shaded under a pine tree, the high walls of the Centre shielding them from straying eyes. His father gave him a tight bear hug, and in that intimate embrace murmured into his ear how much he loved him and how he was sorry for the distance between them. Levi let out a loud bawl as his chest heaved and heaved as if his heart had suddenly become so heavy it could no longer be contained in his chest. He had no words to give. It was sufficient for the moment to lay his head on his father's chest. How had he never realised how tall his father was?

After a while he lifted his head from his father's chest and raised his tear-streaked face to gaze at him. *Was this his father... or someone else?* His father was smiling back at him and there were tears in his eyes too. Levi lowered his head n and spoke to Abba. 'Thank you for the father You gave me, and thank You for changing his heart. Timothy and Mother Adah say I look very much like him. Thank You for my new sister too. I am ready to go back home now. I won't be lonely anymore. I also know that my father will be kind to me. Tell me, Abba, how did You manage all this?'

Levi had not quite reckoned that his father was prepared to wait with him outside until he was perfectly calm. 'Do you feel much better, son?'

He replied with a nod of his head.

'I know you have many questions and think me a most unkind and distant father. Selfish and self-centred. I thank you with all my heart for all the help you render so diligently to your brothers and us. I know that Abba is rewarding you for all your labour of love. I promise you that I will never fail you again. I want to assure you that I love you as much as I love Leah, Logan, and Luke. When we get home, your mother and I will explain better the testimony you will hear today. Especially about how she was pregnant with Leah when we separated from each other. I promise you that we will be truthful about any question you wish to ask about the past. Are you happy with that, son?'

Levi did not want to just nod his head. He was a big boy. His parents were going to confide in him about all the family secrets and treat him like proper family. 'Yes, Father. Is my new sister older or younger than me?'

'She is ten, a year younger than you are. We need to go in now, as that must be the last hymn, and it will be time for testimonies.'

'Alright. And… Father?'

'Yes, son?'

'I love you too, and I am very sorry for running away last Friday.'

'I love you very much, son. Thank you. About last Friday,' Lucas began as they walked towards the entrance of the Centre, 'it was all part of Abba's plan for us as a family to really bond together, as you will find out later when we get home.'

Josef was sure that his mind was not the only one submerged by the goodness of Abba. He was now a father. There was a newborn baby at the Charity Home, but he and Razi had been instantly drawn to the little boy they assumed was a two-year-old but was actually a fifteen-month-old orphan, according to the manager. It seemed, as far as he was concerned, that all the children there were as good as orphans. He smiled, recalling the way he and Razi were like two excited children as they rushed off with their hearts full of expectation, wondering if the right child would be there. The one who fitted their dreams of Samuel.

Lucas felt much better about Josef after hearing all that his wife had told him. As he looked at him now, he recalled his testimony and now felt some compassion for him. He, like most people there, was curious about the young boy they carried. It occurred to him that many people would be curious about Leah too. He gave her a quick glance and could not cease to be amazed by the awesomeness of Abba. Leah was a replica of her mother; a stunning beauty. Even as young as she was, at ten, she was already well developed. No wonder Levi had asked if she was older. She looked fourteen but had the face of an innocent cherub. The same large, sensitive, alluring eyes and delicate facial features as her mother. Then, crowning it all, was her mass of shining black tresses, locks that cascaded down to her hips. She looked as foreign as Eliana did. How eerie can one feel to see one's own replica in one's offspring? Now that he had a change of heart towards his son, his eyes were opened as he saw how Levi too was his image. Even when they were reconciled and he was told this was the case, he did not believe it because his heart had closed. He had thought people were only making these remarks to make him feel better. *Abba, forgive me for all my evil.* He looked towards his son and saw he was already bonding with his sister. His heart was gladdened instantly. They had not made a mistake to rush off to Sidon and find Rebecca, the sister whom he had rejected along with her family because of their link to the family of Judas Iscariot.

If he could accept and forgive his wife, who was once a prostitute, then how could he not accept this lady? She had truly demonstrated the love and faith of the New Creature, and she was his own sister! She didn't consider his wrong attitude towards her but assisted Eliana and had kept Leah for them until they were ready.

His attention was suddenly drawn to Nicodemus. He was the first in their row, followed by Josef's family, and then Lucas jumped, surprised to see his sister Rebecca sitting at the very end of the next row. Their glances met, and they smiled at each other, even though at heart he felt far from calm.

Eliana wondered how much more she could reward Mother Rebecca, her sister-in-law, and her husband, Amaziah. It was true that they had eventually taken over the management of her hotel in Sidon, but she felt she owed them more. She knew that anyone watching her would assume she was focussed on what was happening at the pulpit, but instead she was thanking Abba in her heart for the wisdom He gave Lucas when she struggled with a major decision some three days back. She could see it all vividly in her mind's eye.

It was Saturday, the day after their discussion, just before they set off to Sidon to collect Leah. 'My lord,' she had said, 'we need to agree on some issues before we pick up Leah.'

'Of course! How could I have forgotten? You have not heard my side of the story for those ten years, Eliana. I am so set in the mood to meet Leah.' He paused when he read her face. They did not seem to be on the same page. 'You are agreeable for Leah to join the family, aren't you?'

'Of course, my lord. As eager as you.'

'Then what is holding us back now?'

'My lord, if Leah is to come home before our Levi, I want you to agree with me that when Levi comes home, you will lay your hands on both of them and bless them together.'

'Yes, of course. Parents are to bless their children often as instructed by God and by the Centre. I have not forgotten my duty as priest of this family. Is that it?'

'I am not ready to share the whole of my past with them yet.'

'Why?'

'There is a time for everything.'

'Look, Eliana, what if one of them is told about your past from an outsider trying to be spiteful? Aaron did it to you, and see what happened? No, let us tell them how as a child you were disadvantaged into a life you had no choice over and how, with Abba's mercy and intervention, He delivered you. We will tell them we separated because the devil sowed seeds of distrust, discord, and disunity between us. Because we had been cut off from the words of the Lord and the fellowship of the brethren, we lost each other. I agree that you do not need to go through all the details of the five lives of each of your personalities. No. Are you happy with that?'

'What if either of them asks why I did not come back, knowing I knew where you lived?'

'That is easy! You did not want to be stoned to death! I didn't give you a chance to explain. You assumed you were guilty of deceit and betrayal, Eliana, and that is reasonable enough.'

Eliana thought for a moment. 'How should they reply to people who make them feel bad about my past? I remember how you answered Simeon the Junior. We need to prepare them.'

'Abba will give them the wisdom, but we shall tell them to dust their feet against anyone who would not receive their friendship or their family.'

Eliana thought that Lucas had done the same thing to his sister and her husband, but she had not voiced her thoughts. She would pray to Abba to heal their relationship. 'Yes. But there is something else, my lord.'

'My own story, you mean?'

'Not even that.'

'Go on. Remember what we promised each other when we were reconciled. No secrets. So… what is it?'

'My lord. I want us to be careful about *anything* that will break our home in any way in future. I know there are some people who are divorced or separated physically, and this affected their children. You know, couples can also become separated emotionally, and even if the world does not know, the children will know. Unfortunately, it is children who become the victims of angry parents in a marriage. I know you were very angry last Friday, and that was why you slapped Levi. I have seen you get malicious with me or Levi and seen how you react in those situations.' She waited for his response.

'What are you trying to say, Eliana? After all that we have shared last night, are you still having doubts that I could be insincere to you or the children? Or fall back to the old Lucas? Or be abusive? It is a new dawn for our marriage and family. I know what you are after. Listen and be assured: I am going to be a new father to our son, Levi, and to Leah, just as I am now a new husband to you.'

He watched as she struggled with her feelings or whatever she was trying to unburden from her heart. There was a pause before she spoke again. 'Please, my lord; let us promise each other now before we set off that we will never use our old life or our children as weapons to hurt each other in any way. Especially, to never use our secrets as arrows to inflict emotional pain on each other. For example, you will be breaking my heart if you ever use my past against me.'

Lucas touched his wife's arm and replied tenderly, 'Oh, Eliana, you are so insecure. Why would I ever do that?'

'We are humans.'

He moved closer to her and embraced her tightly. 'I hope you too will remember your anxiety now when you chat with family and friends. I would not like it bandied about that Rebecca is Judas Iscariot's sister-in-law. We may be new creatures, but there are many believers who will ostracise us for this information. Can you also promise that?'

'I love Rebecca and Amaziah very much. I would do anything for them, and I will not do anything to hurt them. I will never deny them, and they will always be welcome in our home.'

'Eliana, we will cross one bridge at a time. Let us carry our cross first before carrying other people's crosses. If it is Abba's will that not only us but other new creatures as well receive them openly, then why not? She and her husband tried so hard to reach out to me during those years when we were apart. I treated them so badly, you can't possibly imagine. Just imagine the life and mind of a lunatic. I got into drinking heavily, mixing drugs in my wine, cheating, and yes, even prostitution… and all other manner of unmentionable crimes. Well, there you go. Now you know how I spent those ten years. In all of it, I couldn't bring myself to hate and forget you. The rest of the story you already know so well.'

Eliana nodded but was still thinking: *Lucas has a very dark secret.* But she did not force it out. She of all people understood that certain secrets needed to wait for the right time to be shared. Abba, who had helped her, would help him too.

'And Eliana, I know you have a lot of wisdom,' he continued. 'Have you ever considered volunteering to lead one of the groups the apostle has been talking about?'

Thank You, Abba! You are confirming to me the thought you dropped into my heart weeks ago. I will leave you to sort out the when and the how. 'As long as you give me your full support and approval, my lord, I am interested. Thank you for your words of encouragement.'

He hugged her again. 'Now, let us go for Leah. Eliana, I am a blessed man. You can never understand the heart this has come from!'

'I do, my lord.' *Now I am convinced he has a dark secret.*

'No, you don't,' he said, laughing.

'Yes, I do! Remember, you have told me all your secrets now, my lord.'

'Well, I suppose so, unless I forgot one… but not on purpose, my beloved.'

'If you could have all my secrets from my past, who am I to not have all of yours from your own past – the ones you mentioned and the ones you didn't? I will always stand by you, my lord.'

'And I by you, till my last breath.' They embraced intimately and, through her gift of discernment, Eliana was now completely certain of a very dark secret in the soul of her husband.

I leave it all to you, Abba, she thought as they stepped out of the door to make the journey to Sidon and Leah.

Eliana brought her thoughts out of the past and back to the present. She was enjoying the service in a new way she had never realised possible. She moved around freely when greeting brethren, without fear of her husband's negative thoughts. She cuddled Samuel to offer comfort when he whimpered, without being conscious of how that might have been interpreted by either Josef or Razi; indeed, she embraced them both and conversed with them. She freely looked for her parents, who embraced her warmly, and she embraced other friends she had once not been so free to embrace. She kissed Mother Abigail and embraced Johanna with tears. She was surprised when Kabul embraced her, but she responded without any misgivings. As she went around, it did not occur to her to keep check on what her husband was doing – he was not keeping tabs on her. So she was surprised to see Lucas and Josef hugging during the greeting time.

Much later, she praised Abba in her heart. The testimonies had gone so well for every person who shared. She could not stop thinking about Samuel. She wondered again whether it was Josef or Razi who was infertile. If it was Josef, she, Eliana, would never have been able to give birth if she had stayed with him! Abba had shown so much mercy to her. Here she was, expectant of another child; God had not shut her womb, despite the kind of life she had lived. Would she have been able to conceive if she had disobeyed Abba and followed Josef? When she had surreptitiously glanced at Josef, he had seemed rapt at Apostle Othniel's words:

'Feed your inner man with things that will help you grow closer to God. Avoid negative thoughts like doubt, fear, guilt, blame, and discouragement, which will take you farther away from enjoying the benefits of new believers. So, mind what you listen to and spend time with people who are positive. Feed your faith with inspiration, hope, confidence, value, and strength. Even if you have made mistakes, God's mercy is bigger than any mistake…'

Josef was reflecting on Nicodemus's testimony. It occurred to him after listening to Nicodemus that half of the people in the Centre were Jews, attending out of curiosity. Also, there were Jews like himself and Gentiles whom Lord Jesus had touched. Many had come there during Lord Jesus's three-year ministry to testify about how they had received healing in different parts of their body. Some had accepted the new faith, like himself, but there were many who continued going to the synagogue. He was certain that some people came because of the meal that was shared immediately after the fellowship. He used to be part of that committee, but he did not know who the current members were. He also did not know those who were responsible for the maintenance of the large auditorium they used weekly. It was owned by Cornelius, a Roman Centurion and a close friend to Jairus, whose daughter Lord Jesus had raised to life. There were some people working behind the scenes to ensure the successful running of the Centre, which was called Bethel Centre. He remembered that Apostle James had said a long while ago that one's service as a new creature was all to the glory of Abba. Abba longed to be close with people and have a personal relationship with them. However, if names of benefactors whom He Himself had blessed were made known to people, they would be distracted and give praise to man rather than Abba. Nicodemus had concluded by saying that a person's soul, mind and body replaced the tabernacle Abba gave Moses for the people in the past. Abba has given us Lord Jesus through His Holy Spirit to dwell within us.

Nicodemus also said that Abba opened his eyes when he met Lord Jesus late one night. Lord Jesus had said, *'Abba so loved the world that He gave His only son, that anyone who believes in Him will not die but have eternal life,'* and He, Lord Jesus, was that light, while the golden *menorah* in the synagogue was only a representation. Lord Jesus told Nicodemus that to get into the kingdom of God, one had to be born again in the new faith, and that was why he, Nicodemus, was present in their fellowship. He testified that he was no longer ashamed or scared to let the whole world know he was a new creature and that he believed Lord Jesus was the Messiah from Heaven. He was not hiding anymore. His life was different now, as he saw things in the light of Lord Jesus.

Josef suddenly realised tears were falling from his eyes. Nicodemus had reminded him of the cruel and gruesome manner in which Lord Jesus had been murdered.

Razi was also reflecting. She had heard the Apostle ask for a show of hands for any volunteers who wanted to offer their homes for fellowship as the Centre was expanding beyond the capacity of the room. She had looked round at that moment and was very sure she had seen Eliana raise her hand. Eliana! Razi's thoughts were diverted from the Apostle momentarily as she wondered how Eliana, who had only recently come to know the Lord, was experiencing so many miraculous blessings in her life: she had reconciled with her husband; she had twin sons; she had found her birth parents and, most amazingly, she had an elder son and daughter who had both been tucked away in safety from the wickedness of the world, protected by Abba all those years she was in prostitution – and now she was pregnant again!

Razi hoped Eliana was not trying to make up for her past with good works. Josef had put up his hand too – was this a spur of the moment decision? Razi loved Josef so much. She had been in love with him long before they became man and wife. His heart had, at that time, belonged to her mentee, Eliana, and Razi sometimes wondered deep down whether he still harboured secret feelings for her. What if they were alone together at some point in time? *Stop being paranoid!* Razi scolded herself. There was no need to feel anxious. She heard Apostle Othniel say he would continue talking to those who wanted to listen, but Apostle James would see volunteers individually. Johanna had put up her hand too! Now she felt guilty. Should she have raised her hand? She had to be realistic: *I have a new baby. We need to bond. Thank you, Abba, for giving us Samuel. We cannot wait to shower our love on this child you have given us. Please use him as a point of contact to grant us many more children. Or else, Abba, who is going to fill up the big house we live in? Abba, You know my heart. Look at all the things I do for You. Listen to my heart as You did to Hannah, mother of biblical Samuel, and bless me as you blessed her.*

Why is it taking so long for my own breakthrough? Why are You not answering my prayers?

Then she heard the soft whisper in her heart: *'My daughter, you were saved by grace through your faith, not through your works! Do not doubt.'*

Johanna was at that same time also querying God in her thoughts. *Abba, You know my heart. You know that I deeply regret my past life of prostitution. Abba, I feel so envious seeing all my friends coming with their families. When are You going to touch my husband's heart? When can I enjoy the feeling of coming to worship You with my husband? When will I start having my own children? I am volunteering to evangelise for You so that You will be pleased and bless my womb and also bring Jephthah to the Centre. Please, Abba.*

Just then, an angel planted a message from Abba into her heart: *'Be grateful, my daughter, that He gives you the freedom to worship here and does not restrict you. However, I have heard you. Can you give him the love he requires from a wife? Do your bit. It won't be long. Love him like Zara did!'*

Zara? But she was a prostitute! Johanna rebuked her mind as she had done several times before when such thoughts came to her. She no longer had anything to do with her past. She was a new creature! If Jephthah could not accept that and went to brothels to find such love, she was not going to be dragged into it. She would talk to Apostle Othniel. There were times the Apostle asked for a show of hands for people who wanted to see him or Apostle James. She was no longer encouraged to wait behind and listen to 'further talk'; it eventually seemed to become more of a counselling session. She wondered each time she saw people's hands go up. Were they receiving instruction to improve their lives?

Father Asher was meditating on what he had learned from the Apostle Othniel, who was rumoured to be Thomas, one of Lord Jesus's disciples, now going by a new name to continue his evangelism in safety. The Apostle had mentioned that Lord Jesus said He was the Way, the Truth, and the Life, and no one could come to Abba except through Lord Jesus. What did that mean? No one talked about Jesus in the synagogue he still attended. He felt that there was no harm coming to the Centre, though, and listening to fascinating testimonies. Abba was great. Every Jew knew that! But was Abba also Jesus? Nicodemus, a strong Jew of the Ruling Council and a Pharisee, had claimed that Jesus was from God because of the miracles He did. In fact, Nicodemus had *claimed* that Lord Jesus was God in human form!

During the testimony session, Timothy wondered at the uncanny likeness between Lucas, Levi, and Father Amaziah's son, Seth. He felt he was looking at a shorter version of his friend. As his thoughts centred on Levi, his attention became divided during the rest of the fellowship session. How was Levi feeling, sitting back with his family? He had cried when his father came and had to be taken out, and Tim felt sad for his friend. He would ask if the ban had been lifted for visits to their home. Levi had been under pressure; he had said that he felt his life was a mistake and that he felt unloved in his new home. Tim had not known how best to comfort his friend, whose life was getting so complicated. He could tell that Levi had changed.

He realised that the transformation in Levi's life was affecting the way he saw life and how he felt about himself and their friendship. Gone was the lively, eager, self-confident, and knowledgeable friend and brother Timothy used to know.

Levi now had a new sister! My, she was a beauty. He would rush off to have a chat with them after the fellowship. His own mother would not mind. She was so amazing – so understanding. He did not have a father, but he felt better than most lads who had fathers. He caught something from the sermon, and he looked towards his mother. She looked wistful, and he realised she might be remembering Lord Jesus. *Why had He died like a criminal?* He wondered again at all His disciples, friends, and followers, and all whom He had healed. Why they had not been there for Him? He became sober and contemplative in his mood. *Was Lord Jesus also Abba God?*

That got his attention back to the sermon...

Leah's mind was so far away from all that was happening in the fellowship. She could have been on a different part of the Earth. She had lost all belief in love. She did not feel like the same person, and she did not know whom to trust. She felt she was living a lie. Her eyes smarted as she thought of her new world. She didn't like waking up in the mornings to discover that this new world was a living reality. Her new parents told her they would explain everything when her elder brother, Levi, returned home from visiting with a friend. She could not believe that the mother she had known all these years had given her away. Was it because she was a girl? Her parents were without a child for five years, and then she came into their lives. She knew love and was very happy with her parents and her younger brother who was born a year later and their sister the following year. They were all treated equally.

But now, she could not bring her heart to love and accept her new family and felt she would not be able to love anyone till she died. Why did her world have to change? Why did they tell her that her life as she knew it was not what she had always thought? She had come to this new, unknown family as a matter of respect and obedience. Her parents had knelt to plead with her, reminding her that they had always told her that the day would come when her true parents would come. She felt tears pushing at her eyes. *If they really loved me, they would have fought to keep me.* They would have spared her the pain of her true parentage right from the beginning. She didn't need to know. She didn't need to leave. Being a new creature was bringing pain into her life. She blinked against the painful sting of her unshed tears as she recaptured the evening her life and world turned completely upside down…

'Let me in to what you are thinking,' her new brother whispered.

'As soon as you let me in to why you were sobbing earlier.'

'Deal,' he said.

At least she would bond with her new sibling.

Rebecca's mind pondered over their giving away the child she and Amaziah had cared for right from birth – Leah. She had cried when they were giving their testimony. Did they do the right thing? Had they unknowingly caused any impact or damage deep in the girl's soul? Leah looked lost and distant, as though she were in another part of the world. Rebecca's heart broke. Right from infancy, she and her husband had told Leah that she was the real daughter of Mummy Eliana and Daddy Lucas, who would one day come for her. She and Amaziah were just Mummy and Daddy Two. Each time the child asked, *'But where are Mummy and Daddy One?'* she had replied, *'They are building a palace.'* And when Leah was much older, she had asked, *'Mummy, am I an orphan?'* Then she had told her the true circumstances of her birth, informing her about her real mother who was hiding away in fear in Jerusalem but had promised to return one day for her child. She would never forget Leah's remark: *'You are the only mother I know.'*

Amaziah knew he was shaking visibly. He had been the last to give his testimony. When he and his wife got back to their seats, she was still crying and had very red eyes. He did not know the impact of his testimony, but he had felt a weight lifted from his heart. He hoped the same for his wife. He recaptured the moment he gave his testimony:

'Good evening, beloved brethren. My name is Amaziah Abraham, and this is my wife, Rebecca. This is five-year-old Seth and Naomi, who is four. We are new in town, and this is our first time here. We are here not to dampen your hope but to raise it by sharing the persecution we have faced and how our hope in Lord Jesus gets bigger even in the midst of rejection, cruelty and persecution. We face trials not because we are new creatures and followers of Lord Jesus but because of the hatred we face from fellow new creatures, Jews and even Gentiles. It may interest you to know that because of our new identity in Christ, Rebecca here was raped by three Jews when she was on an evangelism mission in Sidon, and that was when Abba opened her womb after five years of barrenness and gave us Seth. And a year later, Naomi was given to us.' He heard the silent gasp of the congregation and continued on.

'Look at this scar on my head. I could have died but I didn't. Our home was burnt down. We have had to flee and change our identity, but I am not afraid to be ostracised. I thank God for the courage He has given us to be here. I will now reveal our true identity, and I would like to know on the spot if we are still welcome here to be part of this fellowship.'

Silence fell for a moment.

'If, indeed, we are in the midst of true believers, the real new creatures that have the eyes, ears and mouths of our Lord Jesus Christ…' He paused. 'Right now, we have no home, but I trust Abba to take care of us. He sent us here to share our testimony. We are just being obedient. What is my identity?'

As soon as he asked this, he noticed straight away the tension in the room. It was heavy; even pregnant with what would be birthed by his revelation. However, the atmosphere was not hostile. Tension, yes; but more from expectation.

He cleared his throat. 'Firstly, I was amongst the seventy disciples whom our Lord Jesus sent out to cast out demons and do miracles in His name. We were so successful, and that has been the rock for my faith. Secondly, I am the senior brother of Judas Iscariot…'

He heard unmistakable gasps, but whether of horror, shock, surprise, or revulsion, he didn't know until moments later. Before he could finish his testimony, brethren had swarmed around him and his family, hugging them, shaking their hands, and kissing them. He had not cried, but Rebecca was sobbing. He had seen the unbelievable, and he understood why she was. Maybe it was because her brother, Lucas, was amongst the many who came to welcome them or because Leah had not come out to hug them. Rebecca and Lucas had actually hugged each other, and her brother had whispered something into her ears! It was astounding – a miracle. He would ask her about it later…

There was traffic in the spiritual realm as Abba's angels were busy carrying messages from the hearts of the new creatures to the throne room of Abba. He gave some of the messages His instant approval, and for some of them he reserved it for later, at the right time. The angels hurried to do His sovereign will in the lives of the new creatures.

CHAPTER 7

You are gods; and all of you are children of the Most High.
Psalm 82:6

Let us hold tightly without wavering to the hope we affirm.
For God can be trusted to keep His promise. Let us think of ways to motivate
one another to acts of love and to good works. And let us not neglect our
meeting together, as some people do, but encourage one another, especially
now that the day of His return is drawing near.
Hebrews 10:23

'Congratulations, Josef and Razi,' said Lucas, beaming. 'That was a great testimony. Abba will look after Samuel and give you more.'

'Amen,' they both replied in unison as Eliana kissed the sleeping child.

They were among those waiting.

'If you are waiting to see me,' Apostle Othniel announced in his naturally loud voice, 'please stay in this left corner over here. If you have children, do not worry. We have Sister Johanna and Sister Razi to care for them. There is also, as usual, something to eat for all who are waiting to see me or the other apostles after the general session. Apostle Peter will be at the opposite corner, and Apostle Bartholomew will be over there in that top corner of the hall. Father Jonah will see volunteers in the upper room. Now. I want to know what each of you truly believes about our Lord Jesus. Please think about what you have seen and heard, then kindly let me know if you are volunteering your home for fellowship or if you are here for counselling. I will do the counselling today, and Father Jonah will attend to volunteers. Are we happy with that?'

Everyone nodded.

'Good,' he said at the affirmation of the fifteen people he saw there. He noted Amaziah Abraham and his wife, Rebecca; Mother Rachel, the mother of one of their greatest benefactors – Eliana, who was herself present; and a few other brethren who had given a testimony.

'Do we all believe that Jesus is the Son of God?' He saw everyone nod. 'Good. You see, we all have to be on the same page. Otherwise, how are we going to face persecution? Yes, I ask! Because it will come. It has already come to some of us disciples of our Lord Jesus. Let us not be afraid. Our Lord Jesus gave us authority and power over demons, scorpions, and every form of the enemy when we worked with Him. Why can we not do so now? We can, because He has left His Holy Spirit within each and every one of us. Let us take time to search our hearts and know where we stand. We don't want what happened to Brother Ananias and Sister Sapphira to happen to any one of us here.'

He took in a deep, audible breath before continuing. 'I know there are some of us here experiencing stress, and every day is becoming cumbersome in our lives because of our new faith. Yes. It is persecution, but you will overcome it eventually. You must appreciate the good in others and accept with patience where their imperfection is undergoing construction. We are all bound to have shortcomings, as none of us are perfect, but since the Lord is our shepherd, we lack nothing. Just remember that the new creature has a new mindset: we now possess faith which makes us see that we lack nothing, as David confirmed in the twenty-third psalm. Therefore, let us not be obsessed by our physical needs, possessions, the pride of life, and the lust of the eye, which the devil introduces to the flesh. Let us not be hypocrites like the Pharisees our Lord Jesus condemned, who twisted the laws to suit their own needs and did not exhibit the virtues of God.'

He paused for a moment and looked around at them all.

'As new creatures, do not shrink back into your old worlds. That would be deceiving yourselves. We cannot mix the old way of life, which was ignorance, with the new way of life, which is freedom in our new faith. Lord Jesus said that one can't mix the old wine and the new wine. Remember what He told us about putting new wine into old wineskins?' He saw people nod. 'Yes! You will lose both. Grace and Truth have come through our Lord Jesus Christ. Wait on Him through the new way of life He taught us, and God will strengthen your hearts. Continue to delight in the Lord, and He will grant you the desires of your heart. Be encouraged, I say.' He smiled. 'Now, if any one of you wants to leave for your homes now, that is fine. I have encouraged you all. However, if any would like to still speak with me, I can very briefly pray with you upstairs. God bless you all and grant you your heart's desires, spoken and unspoken, in Jesus Christ's name, Amen.'

'Amen,' the brethren affirmed.

He paused for just a moment as both Mother Eliana and Sister Johanna stepped out with the crowd. *Very beautiful women! Abba, thank You for their faith. Thank You for Eliana. How about Johanna, Lord? Why is Jephthah not here? Why have You not given her and Jephthah a child?*

In his spirit, he heard Abba say, *'Do not worry. I am working in them.'* He heard it loud and clear, and the message resonated in his soul, leaving peace in its wake. He felt calm with the conviction that Abba would give the couple the answer to their prayers.

He went towards the stairs and saw Amaziah and Rebecca already on their way up. As he climbed the stairs, he overheard Father Jonah encouraging a group of brethren:

'…I thank Abba for the new faith that helps us to trust in Him. Abba has accepted us. We are victorious, and nothing should stop us from enjoying His love. The new creature is one who is immovable and unshakeable in the face of persecution. New creatures are conquerors backed by Lord Jesus's authority, so don't let *anything* separate you from Him. Our three dear apostles and I will see each of you individually to hear what you can volunteer, and if some of you here are willing to offer your homes as fellowship centres.'

He smiled as people followed each apostle to a different room.

'Mother!' Eliana embraced Rachel as people around the room exchanged greetings. She saw that her mother had come out from the group of people who had gone with Father Jonah.

'I am so happy and blessed, Eliana! Two years ago, I had no husband and children. Today I have not only a husband but also children and grandchildren, and all my prayers are being answered, one by one.' She kissed Eliana. 'My home could eventually become a centre. I will know next week. Isn't it all amazing?'

'Mother, I know. It is all truly amazing!'

'When can we talk, my daughter? I could come to your house…'

Their attention was diverted as Johanna passed by.

'Wait, Johanna, please,' Eliana said. Then, turning back to her mother, she said in a hushed tone, 'Mother, I will come and see you. I am no longer tied down with the twins. Abba be praised!'

'Abba be praised,' both Johanna and Mother Rachel said as they embraced one other.

'Good, then, Eliana, I will be expecting you during the week,' her mother said.

'Yes, Mother, and you and the family can now visit anytime. You remember the testimony.'

'Yes, but when you come, don't be discouraged by your father.' Rachel blew Eliana a kiss and left. Asher and the rest of the family had already gone home. She sighed. *At least, Abba, thank you that my whole family come out to fellowship with other believers.*

'Johanna,' Eliana whispered as her mother left, looking around and ensuring she was not being surreptitiously watched or listened to. Johanna looked perplexed.

'Where is Jephthah?' Eliana asked.

'Doing business.' Johanna wore a resigned look. 'You know he is not yet a new creature.'

'I know. Don't worry, but please tell him I have a big business proposal to offer him – he would need to come here next Friday to discuss it.'

'Forget it. He won't come. At best, he will wait for you outside the Centre after the fellowship.'

'No, he mustn't. It has to seem we are discussing like brethren.'

'Is that a good idea, Eliana? Jephthah was a former client of yours…' Johanna paused as a red flush of shame crept over the other woman's countenance. '…Sorry. Of course, I didn't mean anything like that. I know you are now living the life of the perfect virtuous wife in your intimacy with your husband.'

'No, Johanna, not anymore. I will not lie to you. Lucas prefers my Dinah personality in our intimate life. Yes! Don't look at me like that,' Eliana whispered softly. 'Abba made me realise that as new creatures, we should be free in our intimacy with our husbands.'

There was a moment's silence.

'You know, Eliana,' Johanna said slowly, 'I thank the Lord for what you just said. Jephthah has become so miserable with our intimate life. It is affecting our marriage…' She stopped as tears welled up in her eyes and her throat felt lumpy and constricted.

'Say more,' Eliana said. 'Is he completely happy with you now as Johanna, or does he miss your Zara personality?'

More silence.

'Please, Johanna… you can be free with me, as I have been with you. I will not break your confidentiality.' Eliana watched as the tears pooling in her friend's eyes eventually spilled over. She hugged her, discerning the abject misery and deep need of her soul. 'Johanna, please be Zara to your husband in your intimacy. It is fine. You will be happy, and he will be happy. Don't be in denial. You will slip several times, as I did.'

'You did?'

'Yes.'

'Oh, Eliana! I have missed your openness and frankness. Our friendship. Let us reinstate the wonderful relationship we once had.'

'I too am eager for your friendship. I miss Razi too.'

'Of course. You must miss—'

They were interrupted by Amaziah and Rebecca and halted their conversation with a secret smile to one another.

'What is keeping our mother?' Leah asked her new brother, balancing a sleeping Logan on her shoulder.

She had learned a lot about her new family and why Levi had been in Timothy's home when she arrived. She liked Timothy and saw why he was regarded as more of a brother than a friend. She felt more at ease now. She and Levi had exchanged their life stories and realised they both had similar experiences. '*Uprooted and replanted*,' Levi had said. '*You will survive, as I have*,' he had further encouraged. '*The most exciting bit is that our parents have secrets they are going to share with us when we are all back at home!*'

'I don't know, Leah,' Levi said now, shifting Luke on his hip and stroking his hair to settle him down. But I hope they don't make excuses when we get home, like 'it's too late to talk'. Remember, we must both insist that we hear it all tonight.'

'I won't forget,' she replied, looking admiringly at her brother. 'Oh… and, Levi… there's one more thing I have not told you. No… two things!'

Levi laughed. He was already in love with his new sister. There was a difference with sisters; he could see that clearly as he contrasted her with Timothy in his spirit. She was so endearing. There was no spirit of sibling rivalry between them. He felt more protective towards her. 'So, what have you forgotten?' he asked, thinking again about how she was the very image of their mother.

'I have this large birthmark on my lower back which Mummy Rebecca said was also on our mother. Do you know about it?'

'Oh, that's amazing, Leah, because I too have it on my lower back!' Levi's handsome face lit with love and appreciation for his sister and how open she was with him. 'I never knew our mother has one as well. I'm going to find out if Grandma Rachel has one…' He paused a second, thinking. 'No. I don't think she has one. I never saw one.'

'It might be faint,' she replied with a smile.

'Oh, yes, I suppose so. And what was the second thing you were going to tell me?'

She frowned and touched her head. 'It's gone... oh, dear Levi! It will come back.' Then, as she saw their father coming towards them, she remembered instantly. 'Yes! I remember.' She drew close to Levi and whispered, 'You look so much like Seth, my other brother. Do you know his story?'

Levi shook his head.

'Leah!' their father interrupted as he drew close. 'It is a bad habit to whisper in public. People might get the wrong impression.'

Eliana arrived just then, and she caught the last words from her husband: *wrong impression.* She wondered why Lucas was already scolding the children so sternly. She decided to change the atmosphere. 'Right! Home time. I have had a wonderful time with family and friends. Have you all had a good evening? Good meal? Good company?'

'Yes, we have!' Levi sounded excited. 'But we are waiting for the best part when we get home.'

'Bedtime, is that? You both must be tired! The twins are fast asleep on you.'

'No, we are not! We are both eager to hear the secrets Father said you and him were going to share with us. Leah said that you were waiting for me to come home first.' He nudged Leah. 'Leah, that's what you said. Right?'

'Right!' she said in solidarity.

'Please... let us get home, first,' Lucas said a bit testily as he and his wife exchanged puzzled looks.

Eliana smiled at the children as they started to walk away from the Centre. 'I am so glad you are getting on so well. Abba be praised. On the subject of secrets, both of you should be polite enough to wait until your parents are ready. Levi, remember I am no longer your sister – and expect you to treat me as your mother. Don't forget that your younger sister looks up to you on how you relate with us. Abba's blessings on you for making Leah feel more comfortable. I see she is not as tense as before and seems happier and more relaxed.' She saw the youngsters make faces that registered their surprise.

'Well done, Leah!' Lucas added with pride in his voice. 'There were moments I was anxious that you would break down and run back to your foster parents.'

'Oh, Lucas, I felt the same fear too,' Eliana said. 'Especially when Rebecca came out to the portico. I was so tense and afraid that I would lose her for good.' Then, on impulse, she turned round and hugged Leah. 'You are my baby. I am so sorry you never knew me all these ten years. Please forgive me. It was never intentional. I thought of you often, praying to Abba to make things right one day.'

To her surprise, Lucas nodded his head in agreement. 'Please forgive us, Levi and Leah,' he said quietly. Levi and Leah nodded their heads, but Eliana sensed their great disappointment about the 'secret telling'.

Lucas took a dozing Logan from Leah and laid him on his shoulder while Eliana relieved Levi of Luke amidst mild, sleepy protests. 'You both go home ahead of us and get settled down,' she said, and the two older children skipped away ahead.

In her spirit all the way home, Eliana felt heavy. The Apostle had first mentioned the concept of restitution in those early days before their twins were born. It was such a long time ago, and she and Lucas had only finally resolved things last week, well over a year from when they were told. How could they expect to do the same with their children? She wished she had stayed back to confide in the Apostle. She felt as if she was going to be stripped naked and face a public execution, and she realised she was not ready. As she looked towards her husband, she discerned his heart was heavy too. What was going through his mind? The task of restitution or his dark secret? Then she remembered Abba. She needed His help and wisdom. What to share with Levi and Leah, whose circumstances had prevented them from enjoying her motherhood for ten years? She prayed for His inspiration.

Abba suddenly gave her a memory of a message shared at the Centre several months ago after her marriage to Lucas. Apostle James had counselled all the newlyweds at the time: Razi, Biliah, Johanna, Amina, herself, and a few others she had not known at the time. What a timely inspiration Abba had sent her! How she remembered this message now, she would never understand. It could only have been from Abba.

She was no longer ashamed or afraid to talk to her children.

'We are home, everyone!' she said in an upbeat tone as they walked through the door, drawing both surprise and hope from Levi and Leah. 'Get settled down and ready to listen to what I have to say to you two!'

'Thank you, Mother,' Leah said.

There was a pause.

'And... thank you, Father,' Levi added, and Lucas smiled. 'Come on, Leah. We are still going to hear the secrets!'

'Is this Eliana, Safirah, Miriam, or even Reubena? It will be interesting to listen,' Lucas thought as he looked at his wife, remembering how she was so against telling their children about her past life as a prostitute. What was up? Why had she suddenly become bold? He gave her a questioning look, but she just beamed back at him. He shrugged his shoulders and followed her lead to lay their twins down for the night.

'My lord,' she said when she had put Luke down, 'please don't forget to lay your hands on Levi and Leah and bless them together, as we agreed. Once you have done that, I will say what Abba has laid on my heart.'

'I am happy for you, Eliana. Like I said, it will prepare them against any attempt of the enemy to sully their happiness or your reputation, should such an occasion arise. May Abba give you the courage and wisdom for what you are going to share. Come here.' Embracing his wife, he continued, 'Remember that I love you very much and I am very proud of you. We are in this together, and let that give you strength.' He released her and saw she was bright eyed and strong. A good sign.

'Thank you, my lord. You do not know how your words have lifted me. Let us go. Can you believe how eager our children are to know so much about us? They call it 'secrets'.'

Lucas smiled and said nothing. He had promised his son that he would answer any questions, and he was ready.

CHAPTER 8

*Come to Me, all you who are weary and burdened,
and I will give you rest,
Take My yoke upon you and learn from Me,
for I am gentle and humble in heart,
and you will find rest for your souls.
For My yoke is easy and My burden is light.
Matthew 11:28-30*

*The righteous lead blameless lives;
blessed are their children after them.
Proverbs 20: 7*

'Levi! Leah! Please come and kneel in front of us here,' Levi heard his father say. They were already seated in the upper room used for prayers and meetings as well as a sleeping room for Grandma Rachel when she used to visit. 'Eliana, join me here, and also place your hands on their heads while I pray.'

The two children knelt, and Levi felt the soft touch of his mother's hand on his head and felt a sobering effect. He wondered how Leah might be feeling. He felt the light imprint of his father's hand as he placed it over his mother's. He closed his eyes as he listened to their father.

'Abba Jehovah. Behold our first-born son, Levi and our first daughter, Leah. We pray Your blessings upon their lives. May Levi be great in the land and in his generation. Like Solomon, may he grow in wisdom and in the fear of the Lord his God. And, like Joseph, may he be a man of integrity. May Your blessings be upon Leah. May she be like Ruth and Esther in her generation. May she be faithful, loving, discerning, and may she have the fear of God all the days of her life. May both of them and their siblings be blessed with Your favour and protection from all evil, in Jesus Christ's name. Amen.'

'Amen,' the rest of the family chorused as they all took their seats on the comfortable, cushioned wooden chairs. Levi saw their mother smile at each of them, as if trying to judge if they were old enough to hear her secret. Eliana discerned Levi's anxiety but knew it stemmed from a fear that she might change her mind.

She smiled softly. 'Well, my dear children, what I am about to tell you was shared by Apostle James when your father and I attended a counselling meeting for all the newly married couples. He told us to never be ashamed of our pasts. He began by saying that everyone had the good and ugly bits of their lives. He said that he noticed that most of the couples there shared something in common with Rahab, who hid the two spies – you must have learnt about her at some point in your groups, yes?'

They nodded their heads.

'Well. There are five women in the bloodline of our Lord Jesus Christ mentioned in Scripture: there was Tamar, who committed incest with her father in law; Rahab the prostitute who hid the spies; Ruth from Moab who was not a Jew and used to take part in pagan rituals; Bathsheba who committed adultery with King David; and Mother Mary who conceived her son with the Holy Spirit before she was wed to Joseph, her husband. These are the ugly bits of our Lord Jesus's family.

'In this family, too, there are ugly bits. I will tell you the story of me, your mother, Eliana, who had the same reputation as Rahab, and how she met Lucas, your father.'

The children stared at her with wide eyes.

She smiled at them. 'So, this is Eliana's story. When she was a tiny baby, she was taken to an orphanage. She grew up thinking she was an orphan. When she was five, she was sold into a life of prostitution. She came to Lucas as 'Dinah' and hid her past and real name from him. Levi, their first child, was two years old when Lucas found out about Eliana's past and sent her out of his home. Leah was already conceived in her womb. She gave birth to Leah and left her with Mother Rebecca, her sister-in-law. Ten years later, she met Lord Jesus who cast out the demons of prostitution and gave her a new life. He also gave her a new mother, Rachel, who happened to be her birth mother! Rachel went to Sidon to find Lucas and Levi. By then, Lucas had already met Lord Jesus, and this made his heart ready to forgive Eliana. They were reconciled, but Eliana did not then tell Lucas about Leah because she was waiting for the right time – which happened just last weekend. That's when they travelled to Sidon to meet Mother Rebecca and Father Amaziah. Leah's foster parents were both heartbroken, of course, to give up a child who had regarded them as her parents for ten years.' She stopped, looking at both children in turn. 'Do either of you have any questions to ask for now? Levi?'

He shook his head.

'Leah?'

Leah looked puzzled. 'Why did Eliana not stay with Mother Rebecca's family and her little daughter?'

'Let me answer that,' Lucas cut in eagerly like a pupil in class who alone knows the answer. 'Lucas and his friends would have found out and stoned her to death as a harlot, according to Jewish custom.'

'But why did Eliana not return two years later, say, and take her baby when it was safer?' Levi asked.

'Because she had already told Rebecca that she would come at the right time. But then she thought God did not love her and had forsaken her, so she went back to her old life. Her home would not have been a suitable place to raise a child in.'

Levi and Leah nodded in agreement.

'Any more questions?' Eliana said. She quite liked the way her story was being taken impersonally, as if it was about someone they did not know. A church children's group story. She felt relaxed and free of tension, with her husband also playing in role.

She continued when there were no further questions.

CHAPTER 9

But I will remember Your great deeds, Lord;
I will recall the wonders You did in the past;
I will think of all You have done;
I will meditate on all Your mighty acts.
Psalm 77:11

'Now, time for the good bits!' Eliana said. 'Eliana only remembers Abba's love and the many miracles God has done for her: how she came out of the slavery of twenty years of prostitution with exactly ten properties to her name...' She noticed Lucas blinking in surprise and elaborated. 'Yes. Three hotels, five houses and two transport companies! Eliana remembers how she was redeemed to become a new creature; how she was restored to her natural family; how she was reconciled to Lucas, her husband; how she found Levi and how she regained Leah. These are miracles she constantly thinks of that keep her soul alive, fulfilled, and happy. Her faith in Abba is very strong and sure. Is anyone sleepy?'

'Not yet!' the children replied at the same time, somewhat indignantly, as if wanting to let their parents know that they were grown up.

'I haven't finished yet, and your father still has his bit to share. Any questions at this stage?'

'Are some of Eliana's properties still used for prostitution?' Levi asked.

'Yes and no, but your father and I will explain that on another occasion when we talk about business matters. God will take us over that bridge at the right time. Tonight is just about Eliana and Lucas's pasts.'

'Alright,' affirmed Levi.

'Is that good with you, Leah? Any questions?' Eliana said.

'Yes. Why did Mother Rebecca not bring baby Leah down to stay with Eliana?'

Eliana thought for a moment. 'Three reasons. First one, Mother Rebecca secretly hoped baby Leah was hers forever. Secondly, Eliana never left any address of where she stayed. And the third one, there was no more 'Dinah', the mother of Leah at the time; Eliana had become 'Miriam' the prostitute… and her home, as we agreed earlier, was not a good home to raise a child. Happy with that?'

Leah shrugged. 'I just find it difficult to imagine.'

Levi nodded slightly.

Eliana reached her hand to Leah's shoulder. 'I know, my darlings. Your parents are not going to pretend that everything will be easily understood by you both or that your feelings will adjust automatically to your new home, parents and lives. We are trusting that Abba, who has brought us all together as a family, will make it work and take care of any emotions we will struggle with.'

She exchanged a glance with Lucas and continued.

'Of course, Eliana too has lots of regrets for those ten years her babies missed her motherhood. She missed seeing her babies grow from months to years. It was a long time. No other baby will ever fill that yearning she feels for you, because each baby is different and comes with their own individual personality. This is what saddens Eliana the most: not knowing everything from all those childhood years of her first two children. She can only get second hand information from Grandma Rachel and Mother Rebecca. So, she trusts Abba to fill up that gap with love, hope, and peace with Levi and Leah now, to surpass those years she missed with them…' She paused, swallowing. '…Alright. I will finish Eliana's story. I hope you both realise that there was every possibility that Mother Rebecca and her husband could have refused to give up Leah or moved far away to somewhere Eliana would never find them. Also, Levi could have been sold into slavery, or any number of other evil possibilities that happen to children when there are no parents could have befallen him.

'Eliana thinks of how Abba is still giving her more children. Right now, another baby is in Eliana's womb – four months old. Even while she lived in sin, Abba blessed her with wealth. So, like Apostle Othniel once said, that which was meant for Eliana's harm, Abba used for her advantage. Not every lady of the red trade is wealthy. Some died of sickness, like Biliah's mother. Some lost their health and then their clients, like Mother Abigail. God was merciful to Eliana. Today, Eliana cannot stop thinking about these miracles. They are constantly in her thoughts. She remembers only her victories and accomplishments. She consciously tries not to remember her hurts, failures, shame, and pain.'

Eliana paused again and allowed silence to fall for a moment.

'I would like you both to remember this day as historical. It marks the day your parents told you their testimonies so that when you look back, you will remember the love we shared. Remember this date today, this night as a memorial one and thank God that you have not had a life like some other children who were abused, turned into sex slaves, or killed at birth because of the reign of an evil king.

'Mother Rachel, your grandmother, lost two sons in one evening and became insane. That was why my father put her away and gave me to an orphanage, where there were people with evil intentions who took advantage of my vulnerability and helplessness. Your foster parents did not give either of you away because of your circumstances like my father did. I was ill, and he thought I would die, so he gave up on me.

'But you have both enjoyed the goodness of Abba; you have experienced love, and your lives have been spared despite the circumstances of your birth parents. Abba found good-hearted foster parents to nurture and take care of you without harm and evil coming your way.'

Eliana stretched, glad the evening was warm and she felt neither drowsy or fatigued.

'I know that you both will undoubtedly miss your foster parents, your life with them and the love they shared with you. You might feel the urge or wish to return – but remember how Moses handled that. He lived with his Egyptian foster parents in the palace for several years until he was an adult, much older than you both. He enjoyed all the wealth, fame, prestige, and privileges of a prince while his natural family were Hebrew slaves; poor, broken, and in defeat. Yet he never turned his back on them. He returned to them.

'Don't ever be like our forefathers who forgot all about the amazing miracles God had done for them, from Egypt to the Promised Land, and returned to idols or had no faith. You coming back into our lives is like coming back to your promised land. You will get God's best. God has shown us as a family His favour and mercy, bringing us all out of difficulties that seemed impossible to overcome. Abba said we should be passing down the miracles He does for us. Don't keep these stories you call 'secrets' to yourselves – pass them down to your children, grandchildren, and great-grandchildren as a memorial of what God has done. Abba has made us righteous. The blood of Jesus Christ has washed us all clean, including those of us who have led a life of sin, like Rahab. Our pasts can never have any dominion over us, ever.' She paused, sighing happily and waiting for more questions. None came.

'As you step out into the world, you are now armed with the knowledge that there are very evil people who do not know and fear Abba. Some people will make you feel like outsiders because of me and my past, or because of your faith and your belief that Lord Jesus Christ is God. Some will be unkind and rude because of your life as a new creature. Remember how, by the grace and miracles of Abba, Rahab was saved. She married Salmon, who loved her despite her reputation, and she became the great-grandmother of King David! So my past should not be any excuse for either you or your siblings to live a wayward life or a life of defeat, failure, and disgrace. There is a difference: You are new creatures.

'Whenever you pray to Abba, as from today, I want you to thank Him for what He has done for me and us as a family. We have received the blood of Lord Jesus on our heads as a blessing and not as a curse. Let us believe in faith that His death and resurrection have paid for all our sins. My sins have been erased. The chains of my bondage to sex slavery have been broken. Now I know joy, strength, peace, love, and the prosperity of the new creature – and there is nothing any enemy can do to me, or to you, our children. My past is no more. In the name of our Lord Jesus Christ, I wear the captive's crown of victory and salvation. We all as new creatures now have power and authority in our Lord Jesus Christ and share in His glory.'

She stopped, taking a breath and smiling around at them. 'Well, my loved ones, this is my story, the 'secret' you both so much wanted to hear. I will end by saying that as new creatures, Lord Jesus Christ wants us to pray and love all who treat us badly. We will love those who are rude or unkind to us. Don't take it personally. Like Lord Jesus Christ on the cross asked Abba to forgive those who crucified Him because they did not know what they were doing, we must also do this. Never forget this, because persecution will come upon new creatures in one way or the other.'

Levi saw that their mother deliberately looked at her husband as she said, 'I will let your father speak now.' His mother seemed at peace.

Indeed, Eliana felt Abba physically take away the burden in her heart. She did not feel naked or shameful, but she realised that she was experiencing anew the blessings of the righteous in Lord Jesus Christ – the blessings of the New Creature: the victory, power, peace, joy, and love.

As her husband embraced her, she saw that everyone was far from sleepy. Leah's eyes were brimming with tears; of course, she had been moved by the gruesome details of her being cast away as a baby and the rest of the story. Levi had taken in all that she had said with his highly intuitive mind. She knew he would be able to discern that which was not spoken, all she had implied which was not explicitly said.

Levi saw her in a new light. 'I am very proud of you, Mother,' he whispered, hugging her. 'You have been as bold as Ruth and Esther.'

Leah also embraced her, saying, 'Mother, I love Mummy Rebecca, but I truly love you now as well. I am anxious that you might think that my love is only for Mummy Rebecca. I too will never be ashamed of you.'

Eliana saw that Leah could have said more, but she had become emotional. Still hugging her and rubbing her back, Eliana said, 'Oh, my daughter, I never forgot the image of you at birth. I love you as much as Levi, Luke, and Logan. Never doubt that.'

Lucas spread out his hands. 'Alright, now, let's all sit down. It must be getting to the middle of the night. I am happy to talk to you both and answer any questions now or tomorrow. Which will it be?'

Before Levi could answer, Leah said, 'Go ahead, Father. We are not babies! We are not sleepy. Mummy Rebecca used to say that we have today but not tomorrow!'

'Very, very true indeed,' Lucas said, shaking his head, his eyes on his wife. Levi followed his gaze, but his father turned his head back to his children. 'I regret the many months I prevented this family from going to the Centre. But tonight, your mother has cleverly brought us to hear some of the messages taught to us at the Centre: particularly the message of love, which is the essential characteristic followers of Lord Jesus Christ must have. Lord Jesus came to teach us about grace, mercy, forgiveness, and the love of God. Abba also wants us to have a relationship with Him. I promise now that this family will never cease going to the Centre or doing whatever Abba lays in your hearts to do for Him and His people. Levi, you will go to school. Your mother has been your teacher, but now in addition you will go to school and become like David and Solomon. Leah, I want your mother to teach you to be like Ruth and Esther and, best of all, to have her courage and strength.' He paused. 'Now. I am not going to preach, but I want to talk about King David for a reason. David has a hundred and forty-one chapters devoted to his life in our Hebrew scriptures! He had a heart of devotion and worship, and God loved him intensely for that. Who would not? Even overlooking his faults! He was once a youngster, like you both, and was mostly ignored and looked down upon in comparison to his seven elder brothers.

'Like David, I was the youngest, of six children in our case, and mostly ignored. Especially as I was born in my parents' old age. My father was about seventy and my mother a little over ten years younger at fifty-eight. They made me feel like I was born accidentally and not a miracle or blessing. I know how much I yearned to be loved by my parents, especially by my father, Levi. I was his image. That's why I named you Levi. Not because I love the letter L, as your mother assumed, but to remind me to never make the same mistake with you.

'When your mother came into my life from Tyre to Sidon as Dinah, I was completely taken by her devotion, love, and worship towards me. I was the most important being in her life. I had never in my entire life experienced so much warmth, devotion, and worth, and my perception of myself greatly improved. Everything in my life prospered, and I felt secure and self-sufficient. I ignored members of my family who criticised my marrying someone who was a nobody and had no family ties. I was completely and intensely in love.

'They saw me as a servant to each of them, helping out when the need arose in their lives. Mother Rebecca, who is the fifth-born, is fifteen years my senior. Our senior brothers are well over ten years older than she is. Sadly, she had no children, and her husband wanted to adopt me, but I refused. I became wild, lived a rough life, I was insolent, and everyone saw me as a reject. Even after our parents died, I never saw myself as a sibling to my elder brothers, who were all married with children as old as me.

'Something interesting happened the year I turned eighteen, when my father passed on. He asked me to forgive him because he had not shown me appreciation and love. To quench his guilt, he left his house to me rather than to his first-born son, Jude, which is against tradition. When my mother died, four years later, when I was twenty-two, she too begged me to forgive her and make peace with my older siblings. Your mother here is a witness. As soon as we became reconciled, your mother advised that I give up the house to Jude as a gift since God had already given us so much wealth and property, so I did. Now my four senior brothers are on good terms with me. They are all grandparents as well.

'However, it was difficult to reconcile with my sister, for many reasons. She was married into the family of Judas Iscariot, who had a notorious reputation. Also, Amaziah's sister was married to a Roman! Rebecca had also gone against my father when she married into that family, so my parents had cut her off. When she could not have any children, we all assumed it was God's judgement on her.

'You can imagine my utmost shock last week when your mother revealed that it was my sister and her husband who had taken her in when I drove her out of my home! Your mother had just conceived Leah, but she had not told me, so I did not know I had another child coming!

'There are evil things I did to my sister which I am almost too ashamed to mention because I hated her so much then and she was dead to our family. About two months after your mother, who was Dinah then, left me, I fell into some very bad habits. I became a drunk, visited brothels, and became violent and depressed. Some months later, even Rebecca tried to reach out to me… and guess what I did?'

No one spoke.

Lucas swallowed. 'I beat her up. I… I started shouting to those around me that she was a traitor associated with the Romans. Some others joined me to beat her. I even lied about her, saying she gave herself to a Roman. She cried calling my name, reminding me we were siblings, and she begged me, but I watched as some hooligans dragged her to a corner, stripped her naked and eventually took their turns and raped her. I left my own sister possibly dying. She was calling out for help in the name of our parents and Lord Jesus Christ…'

Levi felt a lump in his throat and looked round. His mother wore a passive face. His sister was crying. The next thing he knew, his father was breaking down, sobbing wretchedly. Their mother intervened. 'Alright, children, this is enough for one night.'

As if in confirmation, they heard the first cockcrows, muffled by the choking sobs of Leah and their father.

'You can go to bed. I will take care of your father.' Eliana watched until the children were out of sight, then said, 'Levi, I know you're still there. No eavesdropping. Go to bed now and be obedient.' She heard Levi's footsteps retreating, and turned back to her husband, taking him in her arms.

After he had calmed down a little, she spoke. 'It is alright, my lord. Now you no longer have any dark secret that you are hiding from me. You are at rest in your soul now. Come to bed, my love. You are a new creature now. All of that was in the past, and it has all been wiped away. Rebecca has forgiven you. She kissed you. Remember?'

'I do,' Lucas said, but in his thoughts he sank further into darkness: *Can I ever forgive myself? Can I ever let you or anyone know that I partook in the rape and Seth could possibly be mine as well?*

He sobbed his heart out as his wife comforted him in the way only Dinah could.

CHAPTER 10

A false witness will not go unpunished,
and people that speak lies will eventually perish.
Proverbs 19:9

God hates anyone who sows discord amongst the brethren.
Proverbs 6:19

The following Friday, Eliana wondered why she had not seen Jephthah and Johanna during the brethren's exchange of greetings. It worried her because she was hoping he would have at least come to the Centre for the purpose of business. How about Johanna? Maybe they were late and had settled at the very back where they could just about hear the preaching of the Apostle but would be unable to see him over the crowds.

After the service, she was disappointed to see no sign of them. She found herself making other plans as she was making her way home with the family. 'My lord, please permit me to visit my mother. I did promise her last week that I would come. Will you be able to manage for a few hours without me?'

'Of course… we can. Can't we, Levi and Leah?'

'Yes, Papa. We can,' Levi replied, taking Logan from his mother.

Lucas looked at his wife. She looked exhausted. 'But… in your state, I think you should just come home and rest.'

She shook her head. 'I will be fine, my lord.'

Soon Eliana found herself going back in the opposite direction, seeking out her mother in the crowd. She saw Josef, and he saw her at the same moment, but for reasons best known to each of them they did not acknowledge the other. That had been done earlier on during the service. She spotted her mother at a distance and called out, 'Mama!'

Rachel halted and looked back. Eliana had lately noticed a ray of happiness sparkling over her mother's countenance and hoped that she herself might reflect that sparkle now, too – after all, people said she resembled her mother. But today, she realised, her mother's sparkle was dulled. She made her way through the crowd towards her. 'Mama, I hope you are fine. You don't seem your cheerful self.'

'I am fine now that I see you are coming home with me – aren't you?'

'Yes, if that's alright. What of Papa and the rest of the family?' Eliana asked, discerning a burden in her mother's soul.

'Everyone is well. Daniel came a bit late and must have left early. He and his father were arguing over something.' After a pause, she added, 'I did not want to interfere, or I might have been late too.'

'Surely, Mama, you can tell me. I am sure you have an idea. I have been through the worst in life, and nothing can ever make me downcast. I can sense the worry in your heart. What is it, Mama?'

Rachel looked down. 'It is the devil, Eliana!'

'I know,' Eliana played along. 'What did he do this time?'

'Trying to tear our home apart.'

'Exactly what he loves to do! Abba will give you victory, Mama. Do you care to give me more details?'

Mother Rachel was silent. They began to walk together out of the Centre and towards Rachel's home.

'Mama, we have all gone through too much to allow anything to sour our moods. Did you not listen to what Apostle Philip preached today?'

'I did. About Job. It's just that… in your condition, I wouldn't want anything to stress you.'

'Mama, I am strong. Remember that the new creature should have a faith like that of Job – to trust God despite everything falling apart. The Job faith helps us move on. Please, Mother, cheer up, even if you cannot tell me now.'

They walked through the streets together in silence and arrived at Rachel's home. Eliana watched her mother rub her eye against a tear threatening to fall. It made her think of the few times she had cried in her lifetime. Just four times, that she could remember. It was not easy for her to cry.

Her mother knocking the door broke through her thoughts. Basshebeth, Keziah's eldest daughter, opened the door. 'Shalom,' she greeted with a faint smile. 'Come in.'

Eliana followed her mother through the hallway. 'Shalom! My! You have grown since I saw you last. How are your mother and sisters?'

'They are all well. They are in the outer room. It is cooler there.'

'And your father?'

The girl looked at Mother Rachel before answering. 'He was very upset… he left the house.'

'Where is Grandfather Asher?'

'He is in his room. I think he is still upset because he has not come out to eat his mid-day meal, and when my mother went to—'

'Shalom, Father,' Eliana greeted as her father walked into the room.

'Shalom, my lord,' Rachel said.

'Shalom.' Eliana felt relieved that at least her father responded.

'My lord, are you well?' Rachel said. 'I hear you have not eaten, or—'

'This is what I don't like about people who call themselves new creatures!' he burst out. 'Rachel, why are you hiding what we heard from Father Hur? Tell her! You were there, and yet you still go to that Centre where so-called new creatures are harbouring such malicious thoughts about fellow members!' He stared at his wife with a mocking expression then turned his gaze to Eliana.

'Father... please be bold enough to tell me. Mother was too emotional to mention whatever is upsetting her. But I know it is the reason you and Daniel quarrelled and didn't come to the Centre together.'

'I will ask you the question they put to me. Eliana, if you are a new creature, why are you still encouraging other men and women to indulge in prostitution?'

'I don't understand, Father. Please say more.'

'Go and ask Hur and all those Apostles who preach to you on Fridays.'

'I don't know him. Who is Hur?'

'Woman,' he addressed his wife. 'Prove you are a new creature now, and tell us what Hur – son of Ephraim, the senior brother of Ananias, a cousin to Apostle Othniel, and one of the elders at the Centre – told a group of believers and non-believers at the market. Specifically, at Jaza's goat shed. Many of us were there to buy goat milk and cheese. Rachel, tell her the rest!' He made to leave.

Rachel put her hand on his arm. 'Wait, Father! Don't leave. Do you remember that we are no longer condemned despite our past?' She had discerned that it was an issue connected to her past.

He shrugged her off. 'The people who made the comments about you are the very people you sit with at the Centre – and you expect me to be part of such a community?'

Eliana glanced at his retreating back and turned to her mother.

'Eliana, please sit down.'

'Not yet. Let me go and greet Keziah, Bathsheba, Bethany, and baby Batia.'

As she made to leave, Basshebeth held her hands. 'Mother Eliana, do not worry yourself. They will not welcome you. They are the reason I did not go to the Centre. Mother forbade me and threatened to report me to Grandfather. I really wanted to go. I want you to know that I don't share their negative attitudes towards you.'

'Thank you, Basshebeth. Also, remember not to judge your family or anyone. Like Lord Jesus said, we should forgive them instead because they do not understand what they are doing. Let me at least see them and extend my greetings.'

She made for the outer room which was directly under a big leather canopy that shielded them from the sun's intense heat during the middle of the day. Basshebeth waited in the living room to comfort Mother Rachel. *Abba, please reach out to Father Asher and his family. Soften their hearts and let your Light of Truth put away all doubts, fears, and any seed of discord which the enemy has planted. Thank you, Abba.*

'Shalom,' she greeted and made straight to play with Batia.

Keziah snarled at her. 'Go away, you unclean woman! We know you secretly run brothels and taverns where sinners like you attend. You still secretly meet with wealthy clients. Deny it!'

'I deny all allegations and the insinuations being implied, and—'

'Father told us that Jephthah came to tell him to tell you that he would not come to the Centre, but you could meet him as usual, or let him know what you want him to do with the proceeds from *Safirah's Delights*.'

At that moment, Father Asher joined them and picked up his granddaughter. 'Why waste your breath, Keziah? Do you expect her to own up to her sins? Eliana, please leave this house before we get disrespectful. I will ensure that this home will not be used as a fellowship centre, and I am ending the visits from your home to ours starting from now. Now leave!' Batia began to cry, but he continued, 'This family will not associate with teachers and Apostles who are afraid to condemn the sinners in their midst because of their wealth – ill-gotten wealth!'

Eliana sighed. 'Father, don't use me or anyone as an excuse. Remember, in the Kingdom of God a double-minded man is unstable in all his ways. It is not about me. Are you a new creature or not? Attend the Centre with your family and understand what it is all about. You have attended only once, and the devil is trying to prevent you and your family from seeing the Truth. Maybe you do not know that I have had discussions to join evangelism teams to talk to those who are still in darkness and declare my assets for the kingdom of God.'

Asher realised she was telling the truth and saw that she was no longer the old creature. He remembered his argument with his son, Dan, who had said that if a person continued to focus on all the negative things others did, such a person was not of God. He had advised his father to focus on the good and not the evil. He had reminded him again of the miracle experienced by his younger brother, Tobiah, and the fact that God was blessing Eliana. He had pleaded with Asher to not allow anything to get in the way of his faith, and then he had stormed off. That had hurt Asher. He knew that as long as he was against Eliana, Dan would remain hostile towards him, and he didn't want that.

He didn't know if Dan had attended the Centre for worship today. 'Did you see Dan at the Centre?'

'No.' Eliana perceived a shift in his spirit away from antagonism and towards the positive. She could not believe her prayer had taken effect so quickly. *Thank You, Lord!*

'Eliana, give me a chance to be rational. Explain to me your present dealings with Jephthah and what his message means. Follow me to the other room.'

As he was about to return Batia to her mother, Eliana took the child from him and briefly cuddled her close. 'May the Lord's blessings be upon you and give you brothers,' she said, handing her into the strong arms of a smiling Keziah.

As soon as they had settled in the other room, which contained some stools, a table, three beds for guests, and some weaving looms, Eliana began. 'Thank you, Father. I will explain. Jephthah is currently handling most of my businesses, and he wants to talk about one of my hotels, *Safirah's Delights*. When I was Miriam, he used to be one of my clients. But I discerned I could trust him to not cheat me in business, so I made a deal allowing him to buy property for me and use its proceeds to acquire more – and he did so honestly and successfully. Within eight years, I gave him the proceeds of my former business, *Miriam's House of Pleasures*, to acquire more, and he did. To reward him, I gifted him a tavern. He helps me manage my three hotels, two taverns, a brothel, and five houses.

'Last Sunday, I offered one of my properties to the couple who were homeless. There was a man who gave a moving testimony of their persecution and how they had to flee from their home. I volunteered a property, and this is why I had to see Jephthah. I also volunteered to join the outreach to evangelise prostitutes. The Apostles know all that I own. They are praying to God for me to reach out to sinners to receive the light of Lord Jesus so that they can become new creatures like me. I plan to open a school to educate women and use all my properties for the glory of God. I know Abba will direct and guide me at the right time.

Father, I am now a disciple for Abba. I no longer belong to the devil. But it is God who directed my steps here today so I can have this conversation with you.'

Asher drummed his fingers on the table. 'Now, listen to me, daughter – I agree with you. But why do you think it is a good idea to meet with a former client like Jephthah? Don't you know people will misinterpret the situation? I believe Hur somehow got wind of your business dealings with Jephthah. He said those things to ensure that the Centre will not harbour people in their midst masquerading as new creatures. You are not going to be able to explain things like you have done just now to everyone! So, it is a good thing Jephthah did not meet up with you at the Centre. Where is this 'usual place' you meet with him?'

'That was almost two years ago, before I was married and before I became a new creature. We used to meet at my former residence, which is now the shop where Mother works. Or I would drop messages for him at one of the other properties he manages for me.'

'I see. I can understand a lot of things better now. Eliana, please forgive me my earlier outbursts. I take back all the cruel things I said. My family will resume attending, and your mother can use our home to be a blessing to others. Remind me to announce this to the family. However, I would like to suggest two things so that people like Hur and others do not have the opportunity to assassinate your name and character. Since you have gifted Jephthah with a property to pay for the service he does for you, why not engage your own family members to continue your business? That way, you do not have to meet with Jephthah on a one-to-one basis to discuss business – which might be misconstrued.'

Eliana thought for a moment. 'Father, that is very sound advice. I will run the idea past my husband, and we will pray and let Abba decide. I know that Tobiah is managing his wife's business affairs. I think Dan will do well to manage one, but like I said, I must discuss it with my husband first, and then I will feed back to you.'

'Of course,' Asher replied, hiding his disappointment. He had never imagined the magnitude of her wealth and hoped she would consider him to manage one of her properties. 'You know too that you and your family are always welcome to this home. I promise to come to your home to welcome my grandchildren properly. When is the right time, Eliana?'

'Any time is right for their grandparents!'

That very moment, Rachel peeped in, the rest of the family crowding behind her. 'I have just warmed the meal again. Please don't let it run cold again, my lord.' It was obvious they had been eavesdropping.

Asher chuckled. 'True! Blessings on you, my dear wife. I am so hungry all of a sudden. Come on, daughter, let us go and eat. We mustn't starve the little one.'

CHAPTER 11

Fear not, I am with you.
Be not dismayed, for I am your God.
I will strengthen you; I will help you;
I will uphold you and hold onto you
with my righteous right hand.
Isaiah 41:10

Wearing a linen ephod,
David was dancing before the Lord with all his might.
2 Sam 6:14

A few hours after the fellowship meeting, Josef was relaxing in the quiet of his home. He marvelled at the way little Samuel had grown from the small fifteen-month-old baby to the amazing, healthy toddler he held in his arms. Samuel was asleep, but not very deeply, and Josef reckoned the child wasn't quite ready to be laid in the beautiful crib Amina had lent them. Amina's hands were full; her twin sons were a little over two, and her belly was already thick again. It occurred to him then that he was somewhat in the habit of noticing women's bellies! He knew that Eliana was quite heavy and was due soon. He had noticed that his sister, Johanna, looked pale. Surely, she would have told him if her long-awaited child was on the way? But she didn't when he saw her last. She might have been pale for many reasons, so he might be wrong.

Baby Samuel needed a brother. He thought about how envious he felt when he noticed other children playing boisterously with their siblings. Why hadn't God answered his own prayers or those of Razi? He had asked Lord Jesus to bless him with a wife and family. They had one adopted son. Should they get another? Maybe the blessing of having his own children was not his lot.

Samuel gave a sigh, as if to resonate with his father's thoughts. Josef looked at the boy again. They had played together till he fell asleep. It was time to place him in his crib. Very carefully, he rose and then bent down gently to place the child down, hoping he would now sleep the night through.

Unnoticed, his wife had tiptoed from the adjoining bedroom and was watching her husband. She debated in her mind whether to let him know that for two moons, she had missed her regular flow. It was too soon. A month more and she would be as sure as sure. No need to raise her hopes or his. She did not feel pregnant. She never had been, but all the signs and symptoms that she had heard usually confirmed pregnancy were not present. She felt no nausea, no hunger pangs, no urge to relieve herself more than usual, no lethargy, no fuller bust, and no skin pigmentation changes. Nothing other than the absence of her menstrual flow. Even that wasn't a sure indication, she reasoned.

Her husband straightened up, stretching, and she quietly withdrew before he caught sight of her. She remembered that many women could find their flow ceased in seasons of anxiety. It had happened to her once. No – twice! How could she forget? The first time had been when she had gone back to look for her parents, disguising herself as an old woman. She had learned that her parents had died of grief after she had been separated from them. She had gone through a period of depression, and her menses were completely absent for three months. And, of course, when she began to work as a prostitute, she had loathed what she was doing to herself. She had been so tense, anxious, and petrified by fear and terror at what she was involved in, she had not bled for the first two months.

But what was the source of her anxiety now? She knew that the gift of Samuel had temporarily assuaged her hunger for a child. He was still very young, and God could still remember her, or if she was not to be blessed with one of her own, they would get a brother for Samuel at the right time. There were many children looking for adoptive parents. No, that was not her present worry. Her worry was her husband. Maybe that was the reason why her monthly had ceased for two months. What was worse, her worry concerned such a delicate matter that she did not have the courage to broach it with her husband. They had never quarrelled and neither had they talked about each other's pasts. But now, she knew that for them both to be free in their relationship as husband and wife and in their service for God, restitution of a kind was necessary. Especially for him. He was very much in denial.

Josef found his wife in their room, deep in thought. She did not even hear him enter the room or call her name. When he eventually got through to her, she jumped, startled. He did not miss the sadness reflected in the lack of lustre in her usually bright eyes and the pallor of her face. What was she thinking of? *Another child?* Embracing her, he asked, 'Can my dear wife tell her husband what is bothering her so? Or – if this is easier to answer – what has possessed you that you knew not when I entered our room and called your name? I am your husband, Razi. You know you can tell me anything.'

'Anything?' She raised her voice slightly. 'I *know* I can tell you anything, but can *you* tell me the truth about anything I ask you?'

Razi looked at him boldly, her dulled eyes seeming to cast a dare before him, as though they were searching out something in him. He felt their probe, and he was not going to take any risks. 'So, you mean that I am responsible for your present unhappiness?'

'I didn't say I am unhappy,' she replied. 'I am saying that if I ask *you* a question, would you tell me the truth?'

'Of course! Why not? As long as it does not involve our pasts. That is dead. Leave it buried. As new creatures, we cannot mix the 'new wine with the old wine'. Even Lord Jesus said this. Why would you want us to?'

Razi paused. 'What makes you think it is in connection with the past?'

'I know. I don't have to be told.'

'You are wrong. It is not.'

'Another child, then?'

'No, Josef. It is about you and Eliana. Eliana is now free. She speaks and mixes with us easily, but I have noticed that you still feel uncomfortable around her. I don't know why. You do not join any of the teams where she and her husband are involved, and—'

'Can you stop, Razi? This is all your imagination. And I am simply aghast that you have the mind to be watching me whenever she is around. Women are just unbelievable and too simple minded!' He looked at her in shock for a few seconds, and continued, 'What does this all mean, Razi? How can you feel so insecure after our two years of marriage? Why do you torture yourself?'

Silence.

Then he said, 'I think you are envious. God is blessing their marriage with children and not yours.'

He saw her tears and thought momentarily of softening a bit, but he was too worked up. She had the boldness to admit that she had been spying on him! But… deep down, he knew she was right. What else had she noticed? He knew he had cut her conversation short. He shook his head and left the room.

'Josef…'

He heard her call and stopped, debating within himself about whether he should yield. Something prompted him to turn back to their room.

Razi held her hands out towards him. 'Josef, I am sorry if I have annoyed you in any way. Just remember that we are now the beloved of God, and no one can take that from us. Lord Jesus has given His life to free us from every kind of sin, cleansed us and made us to be totally committed to doing good deeds. Josef, feel free to join any of the teams you yearn to join for the love of our Lord. Please live in this freedom we have as new creatures. Put away all bitterness, shame, and guilt, so that you can enjoy the peace of God. As we walk in integrity, God will bless our children. I totally understand what you are going through because I have been there before.'

Josef felt blessed, washed, and refreshed just listening to her. He would never cease to wonder at his wife's spiritual wisdom. It was what endeared her most to him. When she spoke in this way, all his anger abated, as usual. But this time, there was a difference. He knew now that he would join the outreach teams, whether Eliana and Lucas were there or not. He too would enjoy freedom. He embraced his wife and gave her a lingering kiss, but then the whimpering of their son alerted them that his nap was over. 'I'll get him,' Josef offered.

As he rocked his son, he reflected on his status as a descendant of the tribe of Dan. What were the blessings handed down through the tribe of Dan? He remembered that out of all Jacob's children, Dan had been described as a leader… as well as a dangerous snake!

Josef smiled at his son as he played a little game with him, stroking his chubby cheeks. Sam gave him a big wide grin and then dozed off again quickly. Josef gently laid him back down in his crib, thinking about Eliana and Lucas. He was very happy for Eliana, but he envied her husband. Being from the tribe of Manasseh implied a kind of superiority. It included many special blessings – including the birth of many children. And his feelings for Eliana? That was the whole crux of the matter. He was afraid that he still loved her with a burning intensity he feared others might see if they looked carefully. However, he would seize the opportunity to join one of the teams. Maybe then he would see if she felt the same about him.

And if she did? No. His mind warned him not to go down that route.

Chapter 12

*You, dear children, are from God
and have overcome them,
because the one who is in you is greater
than the one who is in the world.*
1 John 4:4

On the Sunday afternoon two days later, Levi was on his way to his father's boating company to collect sales news from Simeon the Junior. He planned to stop at Grandma Rachel's shop on the way to buy some wool and pass on a message to her. Then he heard some shouting and turned round to see some Roman boys arguing over something.

'Let's ask him. He's the one!' they said as he passed by.

Something told him to run away to safer ground where there were more grown-ups and Jewish people around, but then he remembered something Apostle Bartholomew had said which had emboldened and encouraged him. 'You are the son of the most High God, who says, *'Do not be afraid – I am with you.'* He decided not to run after all, remembering that the Apostle had once also mentioned that new creatures had the ability to be who they wanted to be and change the world, no matter what.

'Hey, you!' the shortest but probably the eldest boy blurted as five youths, one or two his age and the rest a little younger, gathered around Levi. He knew they were all confident in the strength they had against him, on his own. He was quite tall but wished suddenly he was very tall and mean looking like Timothy or Apostle John. Even his father looked strong and impressive.

'We know your mother!' they said, interrupting his thoughts.

'Oh.'

'Just 'oh'?' another asked. 'Aren't you going to ask us how?'

He rolled his eyes to the heavens to give the impression that they were a bunch of idiots wasting his time. It was at that moment he remembered the prayer prayed every week at the end of the fellowship: *For the Lord your God, the holy God of Israel, will give up Egypt to free you from all danger and save your life, because you are precious.*

Another broke into his prayer. 'My father said your mother knows how to give pleasures. Can you and your sister also give pleasures?'

Levi felt sick and shook his head. 'Sorry, no. We are new creatures,' he replied slowly.

Another said, 'Can your mother visit me? You see, I am still a virgin.' His friends laughed and booed.

Levi wrestled to keep his voice calm. 'No.'

One of the boys mocked, 'Justus, Kazim's son, lives to remain a virgin!'

'Justus, ask your father for the secret password for Miriam,' another leered.

'She too is a new creature,' Levi replied quietly as he made to move away.

'Stop! We have not finished with you. What do you mean by 'new creature'?'

Levi answered boldly, like one who was older than his eleven years. 'In spite of who you are and what you have been, the moment you receive Lord Jesus the Christ as your Saviour, you become a New Creature. Your old life becomes brand new. So, for example, God will make you see life in a completely different way.'

Levi saw a new kind of respect in some of their eyes, but one of them taunted him. 'Like when you become cowards and do not fight for the honour of your parents? You are a loser! And a bastard, obviously! Tell your mother that we will meet her in one of her taverns she still operates. New creatures indeed!'

They waited for his challenge, but it didn't come, because his attention was diverted. 'Hey, Tim!' he called, beckoning his friend over. 'I am in the middle of my very first time evangelising.'

His adversaries saw an extremely tall youth and, even though they were in the majority, two tough-looking kids made them feel like a pack of five wolves against two unpredictable, menacing male lions. *What was evangelising?* They didn't want to wait around to find out and scarpered away in the opposite direction.

'Tell those guys to wait for what I have for them,' Tim shouted as they ran. The two friends embraced. 'So how did it feel, being in the lions' den?' he asked Levi, laughing.

'As God kept their mouths shut, I was safe. Praise the Lord!'

'You mean they were listening to you the whole time? What did you say that kept them sweet, Levi?'

'Sweet?' He shook his head, his face covered in a cloud of gloom and his heart cloaked in sorrow. 'Tim, you don't want to know. Please don't ask me.'

'Brother, let up. That is why God sent me out at the point I saw you. I was going to your grandma's shop to fetch some candles. So?'

'They abused me. Tried to work me up by referring to my mother's past.'

'I know you have not told me the details, but I heard bits of it at the Centre. It was the reason your father sent your mother away, right?'

Levi nodded. He couldn't trust himself to speak, but he thanked God in his heart that he had remained very calm all through the insults bandied by the Roman youths.

'Levi, I think you should not mention this to either of your parents,' Tim said.

'What if I am asked what took me so long?'

'Let us ask God that they won't ask. Now. *'Thank you, God, for keeping Levi safe from harm when he was in the middle of danger. Please, God, take control of the rest of the day. May it be peaceful. May his parents not worry about his long absence. In Jesus Christ's name, we have prayed.'*

'Amen,' they said together.

After the evening meal that Sunday, Levi found himself alone with his mother. His father had taken the opportunity to enjoy the cool evening breeze as he escorted Amaziah and Rebecca, who had dined with them, home. Before their arrival, his mother had been teaching him and Leah loom-weaving, knitting, and what she called 'the lessons of life'. Levi and Leah were also helping with their twin siblings.

Leaving his sister and brothers in the living room, Levi went to their pantry for a drink, and his mother was there, stroking her huge belly. He found himself wondering what 'L' name would be given to the baby if it were female.

His mother broke into his thoughts. 'Adam, I have been wanting to have a chat with you but have not had the chance to get you alone. Now is convenient. Tomorrow morning, son, after breakfast, your father will be home and won't leave till late afternoon. So, we can stroll out briefly, and you will tell me what upset you this morning.'

'I am fine, Mother. I would rather discuss it with Father, please.'

Eliana sighed. 'I guessed right, then. It is about me. You are being persecuted in some way because of me, yes?'

'I haven't said so. It's a boy thing,' he replied, trying to force some warmth into his eyes. But he knew he had not fooled his mother. She was so discerning.

'Please, my son. Do not tell your father anything that will invoke the spirit of aggression or anger. The human flesh is weak and can fail us in those moments when we are not on guard. That is the moment when the devil seizes the opportunity to strike at us. Whatever—'

'Levi!' Leah shouted from the other room.

They both ignored her. Levi took some water from the cistern and gulped it down.

'—Whatever it is,' his mother continued, 'please don't tell either of us. God has forgiven us much in this house. We owe back much love. Please forgive whoever it is, son.'

Levi nodded as he walked away to help with the twins.

As soon as he left, Eliana felt some slight cramps. It was then she remembered that she had not asked Levi if he had given the message to his grandma to come the following day.

At that moment, she heard Lucas's voice in the hallway.

Levi, back in the living room, watched as the twins ran to their father to be picked up and cuddled in turn. Then his father ruffled his hair and embraced Leah. 'Well done, everyone, for all the hard work. I am sure Amaziah and Rebecca were pleased. I liked the way you all got on well with your cousins.'

'Father, Tim says that Seth and I could pass off as brothers. Do you think we really look alike?'

Lucas didn't reply but turned to his daughter. 'Where is your mother, Leah?'

'Pantry,' Levi answered as he watched their father beat a hasty retreat without answering his question. He wondered if his father still secretly harboured hatred for his sister's family.

If Tim were around, he would ask his opinion about the advice his mother had just offered. He decided to confide in Leah. After all, she was his sister, and he would hate for there to be any reason for them to be distant in future. This was the time to build up a closer relationship. He watched a while as she played peek-a-boo with the twins. She would hide her face behind a table mat and peep over it at intervals, using different expressions to scare them, but it sent them squealing with laughter and he wondered that she did not get tired and bored. If they took the twins outside for a while, he thought, they would get tired quickly or get distracted with other things.

'Let us go out,' he suggested to her. 'Just for a few minutes.'

His sister made a face. 'That will mean chasing after Luke wherever he goes. You know he just loves running as soon as he is out.'

She was right. 'Just for a few minutes, Leah.' He lowered his voice. 'I have a secret to tell you.'

'About what?' she asked, with excitement and eagerness playing all over her face.

'Big secret, Leah. I trust you to not tell anyone. You promise?'

'Of course! Why not help with getting Logan's sandals on?'

Dan was quite surprised when he returned home and sensed a pleasing and calm atmosphere. 'Shalom,' he greeted the household.

His wife and the rest of the family were all in the main living room exchanging banter and pleasantries in response to his greetings. Including his father! Screwing up his face in confusion, Dan approached his wife, beckoning her into their chamber.

'Ah, my son, welcome home!' Father Asher exclaimed, startling him. 'Wipe off that frown from your face and come and hear good news!'

Dan looked round and saw everyone smiling.

'Father Asher, please let me break the good news to Dan,' Keziah pleaded.

To everyone's surprise, four-year-old Bethany interrupted her mother. 'Daddy, please let me tell you the good news! I know. I was there!'

Dan wondered if he was dreaming. 'Alright, alright, you tell me, Bethany.'

'Grandpa has lifted the ban!' she said, aglow with warmth.

'What ban?'

Dan's eleven-year-old, Bathsheba, seized the opportunity and blurted it all out. 'We'd all been forbidden to go to the Centre, but now we are allowed!'

Dan was thrilled and nodded his head to signify approval as he said, 'Praise be to Abba!' He had assumed it was news of Eliana's new arrival.

'That was not the good news I had in mind, Dan. But yes, praise God,' Asher said.

'You have some other news?' Dan asked his father, aware that others were surprised and now curious like him.

'Yes, son. You go and wash up, eat, and then we will take a stroll and talk man to man.'

'My lord, are you free?' Eliana asked her husband as he entered their room, searching his face.

'Depends.'

'Just want to know if you can spare a few minutes. I want to run something by you.'

'Meaning?'

She looked at him more closely. Why was he on edge?

'Business talk. I have spoken to you about my past, but I have not discussed the business part. Now or later?' She saw he couldn't make up his mind. Something had upset him. 'My lord, what is it? Did your sister say anything while you were out with them?'

How could he ever talk about that frightful, abominable part of his past in connection with Rebecca?

'No,' Lucas replied, 'they were still amazed at how God had brought them to a place of rest, love, and acceptance at the Bethel Centre. They never imagined that they would be given lodgings at such a very low rate.'

Eliana patted the bed next to her. 'Come and sit down, my lord. God is doing wonders. I told you of how God gave my father a change of heart towards me and wants to be involved in my business. I told him to wait until I discussed things first with you.'

'Now you have my ears. But wait… it is rather quiet in the living room… I'll just check the children and will be right back,' he said, turning out of the doorway. He had not forgotten the question his son had asked him. He should have laughed it off. He would find a way to amend his mistake.

Where were the children? He was not surprised that they weren't in the house, but he was very surprised that they did not ask permission. How many times had they been warned to stay indoors? The enemy was out there waiting to pounce on followers of the new faith. Any small excuse could start off a street fight, and innocent people often became victims. He rushed out and became even more anxious when he could not see them playing at the front of their home.

Trying to stay calm, he went round to the back. There they were! They had not even seen him. Some other children who were also out enjoying the cool evening breeze were playing with the twins. What was Levi telling Leah? She looked tense and frightened, and he clearly heard her ask her brother, 'What if Tim had not come?'

Just as he was trying to make out what was being said, his wife came outside and immediately called the children to bring in the twins. Then she turned around slowly, holding her stomach with her right hand.

Lucas saw Levi smile as he went to round up his brothers, but Leah looked very worried. 'Everything alright, Leah?' he asked.

'No, but I can't talk about it,' she said.

'You can't? But can you pray about it? You know how Abba loves hearing prayers from children.' Lucas turned to help Levi, taking hold of Luke's hand. He stopped, studying his eldest son for a few seconds. 'Leah... Levi and Seth do look alike, don't you think?' He saw Levi smile.

'Yes, I noticed that the first day I saw him,' she said.

'I am not surprised,' Lucas said. 'You know my sister and I take after Grandfather Levi in looks. So, it is not surprising for our children to look so alike. Now, how about you, Levi? Are you going to be man enough to tell me what Leah cannot tell me? I overheard what she asked you. She is worried and says she can't tell me.'

Levi paused. 'It is a big secret, Father. But... I am willing to trade it in exchange for something from you. Man to man,' he replied cheekily.

'Anything for you, my son. Why don't you follow me to the office tomorrow after your grandmother arrives?'

'Deal, Father.'
'Deal, son.' They clasped hands.

CHAPTER 13

*Therefore, as God's chosen people,
holy and dearly beloved,
clothe yourselves with compassion, kindness,
humility, gentleness, and patience.
Colossians 3:12*

Razi felt refreshed after her evening bath. She felt greatly armed with a better strategy to face her husband. She felt strengthened; maybe because today was Sunday – a day of peace. She went through their conversation. One thing was clear: he did not want them to bring up their pasts. She had to find a way. She remembered Abba and decided to confide in Him. He had been an ever-present help when she confided in Him or put a case before Him.

She was strengthened by words of encouragement from a courage angel on guard, speaking Abba's words directly into her soul: *'Come boldly to the throne of God, and you will find help and mercy.'*

Abba, I am going to trust You. I am going to believe in faith that you have blessed my womb with children. I am going to tell Josef about the wonderful thing You have done for us. Please, Abba, I come to Your throne for Your help and mercy. Give me the *confidence to speak of my past with Josef. Let him listen and not turn away. Rather help him to open up and speak of his own past too.*

She felt bolder after praying. Abba, who had dealt with the shame she felt expressing her desires to her husband, would certainly take care of this marital issue between them. Abba would also help Josef to feel free to visit people without any guilt from his past. Why was he still scared? What if in their intimate moments it was Eliana he was thinking of? *Abba, please shrug off this anxiety.* She was going to depend on Abba's mercy and help this night. Lord Jesus said if they had just a little faith, as tiny as a mustard seed, it was enough to command a mountain to be thrown into the sea.

'You are out of the bathroom?' Josef cut through her thoughts with his sudden appearance.

'Yes. Were you looking for me?'

'No, no... actually, Sam is sleeping, and I came back so we could continue chatting.'

This was her chance. As she put on her nightwear, she said, 'Let's hope Sam is asleep for the night. He ate well, didn't he?'

'Yes, he did.'

'Are you going to wash too?' she asked, the soft hue in her voice reflected in her eyes.

'Good idea.' He added in his thoughts, *'Loosen your hair while I go and wash.'*

'When you return, Josef, I have the best news that will gladden your heart this night.'

'If it is a testimony from the Centre or your bakery, let it wait till after,' he said as he slipped away to his favourite wash room.

Razi took the opportunity to peek in on Sam, who slept in his cot in the adjoining room. All her maternal warmth and love swelled in her as she watched him. God was good. God was going to give Sam a sibling. What did she ask God for? Sometimes she asked for a daughter, and sometimes she asked for twin sons.

Other times, a brother for Sam. She believed that if God could give Eliana twins, then He could do the same for her.

She returned to their room and prepared herself specially with a deviation from her own style. She heard Josef's footsteps approaching their room and placed herself in a shadowy corner so he couldn't see her face. 'Which should I serve you first: the news or Eva's story?' she said as he entered. An odd expression came over his face, and the next thing he said made her realise that he had misunderstood her.

'Eva first, of course. You should have loosened your hair so that as you dance, you could use your hair to tease me. Hurry, Eva… don't keep me waiting,' he said in the silken voice of his former self, Jocheb. He lay down on the bed in his loin cloth.

Razi decided to play along. Abba was in this. She would trust Him. 'Alright,' she said coyly, 'be a good boy, Josef. Face the wall and close your eyes…' she shook out her hair, '…and stay that way till I tell you to turn around.'

She became Eva again. When she was ready, she stood nude before her husband, unabashed when he eagerly opened his eyes at her command. Josef saw his wife transformed. Her lips were red, and her eyes had been heavily pencilled into alluring black slits. Her hair cascaded over her full breasts. She could see how pleased and excited he was. She knew she was not as beautiful as Eliana had been when she was Miriam, but she sensed that the desire he felt was matchless. She saw it. She felt it. She was overwhelmed by it. She had given him a new mental image to cover the past one. She was tempted to ask that they exchange their past stories, but she felt a restraint she herself didn't understand.

'Come to me, my dazzling, dearest, beautiful Razi. I never imagined you could give me what I wanted at this cost to yourself! What a sacrifice. After all this, my treasure, I too will give you my good news.'

'My beloved, I am happy to make you happy. It gives me joy. Believe with all your heart that this is your Razi, for you alone and never for anyone else. Do you want me to dance now, my beloved?' She saw his hesitation as he battled between the choice to have her there and then or to watch her dance.

'Why not, my dearest treasure?' he whispered with longing, his Adam's apple quivering in his throat. Razi began to dance to music which only she could hear; an angel melody. She did not know how long she had been raptured in that state of complete euphoria when her husband grabbed her and gave into her as he never had before, connecting them together in a new way. As they sank deeper and deeper into the abyss of their love, both knew that a new era in their marriage had been born.

Johanna and Jephthah came home rather late after spending Sunday visiting other brethren. They had visited Amina and Tobiah and then spent the rest of the evening with Mother Rachel and her family. To Johanna, this was her time with her husband, since he did not go with her to the Bethel Centre even though they could not worship together in the temple because in the eyes of the Jews there they were still outcasts.

She knew Jephthah was happy to fulfil her desire for them to have Sundays together and be seen by their friends and fellow brethren together as a couple. She heard him whistling on his way to their washroom. A lot of things fought for her attention as she went into her own personal bedroom to undress.

Now that she was alone, she opened the door for the spirit of gloom to possess her being. She had felt it lurking and had tried to suppress its feeble knock at her heart. For so long she had ignored it, trying to honour Abba who had been so merciful.

There she was – Zara the prostitute transformed into Johanna the new creature. She had given up one of her properties for almost next to nothing to start a fellowship centre at the other end of the city to make life easier for brethren from that area. Large crowds could draw unnecessary attention.

Two days ago, at the Centre, she realised how acutely miserable she felt without her husband beside her. She had noticed that Mother Rachel and her entire family had begun to attend, though she noted their absence at the last meeting. All her friends were present with their entire families. *What an irony!* Since Abba had performed the miracle of making her a new creature, she had done good works for Abba. She had been kind, generous, had forgiven her mother, changed her name and continued to support the needy in their community.

Abba had been faithful, bringing her from the lowest pit to a place of grace, acceptance, love, and unity with other new creatures. She did not hope for a child. She knew that all things were possible for Abba, but He had done great miracles in her life, and she seemed content. She was no longer young. She had suffered three abortions and had contracted a very severe disease which, she had learned, had eaten up her womb. Her main desire was for her husband to become a new creature. After that, they could adopt as many children as they wanted. It was unfair to bring up a child whose father was not a new creature. Such a marriage would not last. The Apostles talked about unequal yokes. To her, this meant that marriage thrived best when both couples were of like minds.

Her husband called to her that he was through with his night bath and would be waiting for her. She knew that he would have realised she was in a poor mood when she entered her private bedroom, but still, to her surprise, he called out to her. She did not answer him. He was the main cause of her anguish.

'Johanna, my daughter, your husband is calling you,' her mother, Abigail, announced from the room next to hers. Soon, Johanna heard her footsteps. *Faithful Mother. Coming to find out what is amiss after a great evening.* On the surface, Johanna had been in high spirits; lively, chatty, and exhibiting a healthy appetite. How could things have turned for the worse as soon as they stepped indoors? Her mother was probably perplexed.

'Johanna?'

'Mama.'

'What is it, my daughter?'

'Nothing, Mama. Please go and have your rest. You should be used to my moods now. I am going to pray, and I will be fine. Please don't bother.'

Mother Abigail was not easily deceived. 'At least go and fulfil your wifely duties to your husband. Then you can come back here and have all the time you want to yourself. Don't forget that the enemy of the new creature is looking for who to accuse before Abba. If you don't go now, you will be accused of disobedience. Worse, your prayers will not pass the ceiling of this room. So go, my daughter.'

'Johanna,' Jephthah called out again.

She consciously suppressed the feelings of disobedience, pride, anger, irritation, and stubbornness. 'I will be with you shortly,' she answered as she gave her mother a knowing glance: *anything for the pleasure of my Abba through Jesus.*

She made for the washroom attached to her private bedroom and hastily washed herself. The memory angel saw that Johanna had submitted to the Spirit of peace, humility, gentleness, obedience and kindness, all for the sake of Jesus, to God's pleasure and glory. A divine memory of the past was deposited to work in her thoughts, and this instantly dispelled the spirit of gloom.

So, my husband desires me this night… and not for the want of a child. Just me. Me. She remembered her conversation with Eliana, who made the choice to be Dinah in bed with her husband. Yet God had blessed her and was still blessing her. *Why not?* she asked herself. And then she remembered something else: *'My daughter, you were saved by grace through your faith, not through your works! Do not doubt. Can you give Jephthah the love he requires from a wife… like Zara?'* She suddenly sensed feelings of desire and wanted to enjoy sexual pleasure in a way her body had wanted for a while but which she had intentionally refused. She embalmed herself with a heady oily perfume, which left her skin shiny and silky looking with a glossy feel. Then she let loose her hair, oiled it with the same perfume and piled it into high twists on her head. She walked stark naked into their room, lit a candle and whispered seductively to Jephthah, 'I am ready for you, my husband. How do you want me to pleasure you?'

'My God, you are real! Johanna is truly a new creature. This is a miracle!' Jephthah exclaimed.

She smiled as they both entered the world of pure marital love. They had been set free. The answer to Apostle Othniel's prayer was answered that very moment.

'This miracle is permanent, my husband. I have missed the real you,' Johanna said a bit later.

Feeling overwhelmed by what had just transpired between them, Jephthah decided to share his thoughts. 'Oh, my darling Johanna. Is this forever from now… or are you doing this as a favour in return for something?'

She smiled softly. 'No, my husband. Abba confirmed His word this night. I remembered something that came into my mind about four-and-a-half months ago about feeling free with you in our lovemaking, as I used to when I was Zara. I dismissed the thought because I thought it was my own mind, my weak flesh. This night, out of the blue, comes this same thought again.

That was Abba confirming His Word. I am so happy and sorry to have denied you your pleasure as well. All these months, I merely wanted to be pious.' They both laughed.

'My dear wife, let me tell you excellent news that will gladden your heart right now.'

'More pleasures? Bring it on, my husband!'

'No, listen. This will blow your mind because it has blown mine.'

She sat up with an apprehensive look that equalled his own. She was now worried. Her husband had called her three times, and all she had thought about was sex. *Typical,* she admonished herself.

'My darling, I know you are aware that I still visit brothels occasionally.'

This is it. There is another wife… or some child from another woman…

'It is not that I want to deliberately hurt you. When I find myself under sexual pressure to assuage the longing you have not been able to satisfy, then it happens. But tonight, during my wash, I engaged with God in my mind. I told God that I wanted to have you like when you were Zara, and then I would no longer visit brothels—'

His wife broke in. 'Abba! Abba! Forgive me for ever doubting You. You are faithful. You love me very much. I am your beloved…' She felt her husband embrace her as she succumbed to her emotions.

'Wait, that is not even all, Johanna. I never imagined that what happened this night would happen in this lifetime. I wanted to further justify myself for visiting prostitutes if you refused to give me love as you used to. So, guess what I said next?'

'My husband, I am so beside myself with elation and joy. God has performed so many amazing miracles that I cannot be surprised at the impossible right now.'

'Well, you will be! I told God I would even become a new creature too and follow you to the Centre this coming Friday if you could be Zara in bed with me! I never imagined God would answer me. Johanna, I mean to keep my promises to God.'

'Alleluia, alleluia!' Johanna shouted into the night, elated. Jephthah was right. This had surprised her. She could only offer praises to the God of the impossible.

From Mother Abigail's room, they heard an echoing shout: *'Alleluia, alleluia!'*

Eliana sensed that her husband had something on his mind as she lay on her side of the bed as comfortably as her swollen belly would allow. He came into their room with a worried expression written across his face. 'Are the twins asleep now?' she asked, merely to encourage him to unburden his mind.

'Just Luke, but Logan will be very soon. You said you wanted to talk business with me. Are you very tired or sleepy?'

She was, but for his sake she said, 'You go first. Sunday is not far gone yet. What is on your mind, my lord?'

'I don't want to discuss it with you if you are sleepy, Eliana. It is about Levi and Leah.'

'Oh, yes…? Please tell me. I am not too tired.' Her voice must have shown her eagerness.

'You know our son better. Did he tell you anything unusual today when he returned from his errands?'

'No, but why?'

'Something is not quite right. And I fear he may have been bullied or got into a fight… or just something unpleasant,' Lucas said slowly.

'Why would you think that?'

'Levi told Leah something that got her worried. Anyhow, you mustn't worry. I hope to find out tomorrow when we go out. As soon as your mother arrives, I will take him with me.'

'But my mother will need his help, and Leah's too. Why not wait until our child is born?'

Lucas sighed. 'We shall see. And the business talk?'

'Yes, my lord. Now that I am married, I don't need Jephthah looking after my business for me.'

'You said your father wanted to take it on?'

She nodded. 'What do you think? Right now, Jephthah is helping me manage two hotels and four houses in Jerusalem. Father Amaziah and his wife took care of the one in Sidon, but they have now left Sidon. We may need to sell it and use the proceeds to buy more property here in Jerusalem. Like a travel lodge. I sold the inn in Samaria, which helped to acquire some of the property I bought here in Jerusalem.'

Lucas stroked his chin thoughtfully. 'This is what I will advise you. It is a good idea to leave the Sidon hotel. I can travel occasionally to supervise that for you. Father Asher and Dan are very involved with their carpentry and husbandry business – unless, of course, they can take turns in the supervision. For now, I will meet with Jephthah on your behalf and get him to show me all the business details and proceeds for each property. After this, we can make some decisions. In fact, I have been thinking that Levi is old enough to start learning about my boat business. Simeon the Junior was his age when he came to work for me.'

'Thank you so much, my lord. It is my wish that my business becomes a family business and none of the hotels will run as brothels any longer.'

'One more thing, Eliana. This is not to hurt you, but I need to know. Please tell me the truth. Did you sleep with Jephthah?'

'No.'

'I don't believe you. How did your relationship begin with him?'

Silence.

'I am sorry. I should trust you.'

'I told him that if he proposed to my friend, Zara, and married her, he could manage my properties for a twenty percent share.'

'Where did you meet him?'

'He was Zara's friend. I mean… Johanna's.'

'Does Johanna know about this matchmaking?'

'No.'

Lucas thought for a few moments. 'Did you sleep with Nebo?'

Eliana sighed. 'You promised that you would not ask these questions.'

'I promised that I would not use your past life to insult you, hurt you, or start a quarrel between us. Right now, I need to know everyone we know whom you have had an affair with. So… did you sleep with Nebo?'

'No.'

'Tobiah?'

'No. My lord, please stop. You are hurting me. You are using my past to inflict pain and shame. I feel humiliated. Please leave my past buried. I am a new creature!'

Lucas shook his head. 'Actually, I've changed my mind. I don't want to meet with Jephthah, and you *know* why. I give my permission for your father and brothers to help you. Leave me out of things. When our children grow older, they can take over. Goodnight.'

'Goodnight.' Her husband was tense, and his mood was slipping down to a poisonous place.

She had to pray.

Levi had heard the whole conversation. He tiptoed quietly back to his bed. His father was being unreasonable. Did he forget that she was a prostitute before, or did he not know what prostitutes did? He made up his mind there and then that he would not tell his father about his encounter with the Roman boys. By tomorrow, surely his father's mood would make him forget that they had made a deal to swap secrets.

'Dear Abba,' Eliana prayed, *'forgive me for the lies that I told to my husband. I did it for the sake of peace. I know that he knows I lied. Please do not let this become so awkward between us that our marriage deteriorates. My heart is heavy. I can't pray. Help me, Abba.'*

Then she heard the whisper: *'Be at peace, daughter. Put his hand on your tummy, and soon after that, help him relax.'*

God knows best, Eliana thought to herself. She obeyed. She reached for her husband, who had turned away when he bade her goodnight. It was difficult to get hold of his hand. *Abba, get him to turn.*

He did not turn. So, kneeling up, she massaged his back. He turned to face her, and she took hold of his hands and laid them on her belly.

'It is quite taut,' he said.

'Yes.' She adjusted herself with pillows until she was comfortable. Soon she began to massage her husband gently in the place his tension would be released…

'Forgive me, my darling,' he said a little later. 'I crossed the line. Old wine does not belong in new wineskins. I will talk to Jephthah. I just wish he were a new creature too.'

'I forgive you, my lord. All the brethren are praying for Johanna and Jephthah. I have faith. God will answer at the right time.'

The angels on guard blessed them with a peaceful, deep sleep.

CHAPTER 14

*For sin shall no longer be your master,
because you are not under law, but under grace.
Romans 6:14, NKJV*

After their lovemaking, Josef blew out the candle. He did not feel sleepy, but he was not keen on rekindling their passions. He wanted to tell his wife that she was an incredible woman and that he felt he had been divinely visited. He knew that she, too, was not asleep. Now that he was fully satiated sexually, he realised that he was in no mood to please her by sharing the sordid stories of his past. Why mar such a lovely Sunday night as this? He would commend her instead.

'Razi, my love. You are truly a remarkable woman. Look what you put yourself through just to please me.'

'Josef, it was a joy, and I am going to keep it this way.'

'Thank you so much, my beloved. That would certainly be heaven on earth. I wish I deserved such a privilege. Can I ask for an additional favour?'

'Anything for my husband – and you are deserving of it all.'

'Please can you always call me 'beloved' instead of Josef? It makes me feel really special.'

She laughed softly. 'I just made up my mind that this was what I would start calling you! What a coincidence. I am so glad our minds are working as one.'

She remembered that he had said he also had good news to share, but she was not going to rush him. Her own news might wait too, she thought as she felt fingers of doubt begin to tug at the edges of her heart. She struggled with faith and doubt.

'My beloved,' Josef said after some moments of silence, 'you said you had good news for me. I am far from sleepy, you know.'

Faith won. 'Alright, my beloved. God has given us a new addition to our family. It has been three months now.' *Done. Just like that!* 'And your good news?'

Josef stared at her. 'Wait… my beloved! Did you just say that we have been blessed with a new arrival?'

She laughed and repeated the good news.

Her husband got off the bed, lit their oil-lamp and peered into her face. She was not joking. 'My beloved Razi, why would Abba even bother about me? Do you know where Abba picked your husband from?'

'Abba works His miracles in ways we can never understand. I have long ceased to be shocked. He is the God of Miracles. Remember? Please tell me!'

Nodding his head, he drew closer to his wife and started talking about how he had been a prostitute and slept with other men.

At the end of his life story, he felt his love for her take on a completely new light as she embraced him and said, 'I am truly very proud of you, my beloved, and I am more than securely convinced that you love me.'

'You mean, you are not shocked, ashamed, and disgusted about my relationships with men like Yosey Uriah?'

She shook her head.

'Had you then known I was a male prostitute before?'

She shook her head again, all her love expressed in her eyes.

'So… when I turned you to take you by the back, did you wonder?'

She shook her head.

'My love, you can now understand why I was so obsessed with Eliana. She knew what I really was and yet was not put off. I am now completely free, finally and forever. Abba has touched me this night. I can face her without any fear of feeling uneasy due to my past relationship with her. I can also be open with you about *anything*, Razi.'

'I am so happy for us, my beloved,' she said.

'Now, my beloved wife, you have told me you were an only child of slave parents and how your life took a turn for the worse after being separated from them at just twelve. I know that led you into prostitution until Abba saw fit to send Father Simeon into your life with the Word of God. He finally took you to Lord Jesus, and you never looked back. Anything else I don't know?'

'No, my beloved. I laid most of it out that first night of our marriage and gave more details over the first week. In fact, I am happier with you confiding your life story to me than the news of the new blessing God has given us. It was like an invisible barrier between us.'

'How so, my beloved wife?' he asked in surprise.

'Listen, my beloved. This night, you spoke of a divine visit. You have just renewed your faith by sacrificing your fears and trusting Abba completely. Now, you understand the power of grace and that you are not to sin under the excuse that God will forgive you if temptation causes you to dwell on sexual thoughts of Eliana. Beloved, I am so glad! You would have been an easy snare for Satan.'

'My beloved wife, you are quite right. I knew deep down that Eliana had given herself completely to Lord Jesus. I could see that she allows Him to work in her and that she has the desire to do whatever pleases Him. I confess that I used to submerge myself in sexual fantasies of being with her. But now, by the power and grace of Jehovah, I submit my will over to Him and will never harbour the desire to do such evil… or anything else that displeases Him. What brings tears to my eyes is that all the time I was harbouring the craving to be with Eliana, it still pleased Abba to bless us. *Oh, Adonai, You overlooked me taking my liberty as a licence to sin. You are indeed merciful. I can't receive Your mercy if I am not repentant. Oh God of a hundred chances, have mercy on me yet again, and thank You so much for adding to my family. Thank You so much for my beloved wife, Razi. She is the perfect gift You gave me. How can I show appreciation?*

He sobbed on his wife's chest.

At that moment, angels sent by Abba placed His Word on Earth to benefit those that needed it:

I am the Lord; I do not change.
Whoever endures to the end, shall be saved.
Make the most of every opportunity;
don't be vague and thoughtless,
but live accurately and purposefully.
Do not fear, for I have redeemed you.
I have summoned you by name; you are MINE.

Every member of Bethel Fellowship Centre received the Word into their spirits and were blessed.

Soon Josef was so deeply asleep he did not even stir when Razi gently moved his head from her bosom. Just as she was about to settle for the night and savour her blessings, Samuel cried out briefly. She was not alarmed. All babies cried or laughed in their sleep. As she reached his cot, his cry turned into a smile. She gently adjusted his cover cloth and went over to her husband's side of the bed. From the psalms, she prayed the prayer, *'The earth is full of Your loving kindness, Yahweh.'*

In the household of Tobiah and Biliah, Sunday had been different. The entire family had spent the whole day with Father Asher and the family and then returned home late in the evening. After Abel, their five-year-old, and Reuben, their two-year-old, had been put to bed, they had their night bath, knelt together and held hands. Tobiah prayed: *'Abba God, Biliah and I are very happy with You. Dan left this house a very troubled man two days ago. But when we visited him today, You had gone ahead and made all the crooked paths straight. You even restored the relationship between our sister, Eliana, and our Father! Thank you for the lovely meals and time we spent there. It is good to know that Father and the entire family will always attend the Centre. Thank you for this night and tomorrow. Please send your angels to watch over all your people and all our loved ones. Abba, we trust in You. You are our God always. Blessed be our Lord Jesus Christ, Amen.'*

'Amen,' Biliah agreed.

'Ah, my love, I need to be very gentle with you this night,' he said with twinkling eyes.

'Yes, my love. We must be more careful now that I have started to feel the baby's movements.'

'I promise to be very careful, my darling. I don't want to hurt our princess.'

'How do you know it will be a girl?'

'Male and female created He them. He has created the males.'

She laughed her throaty laugh, the one she knew always excited her husband. He was so humorous; it was what had attracted her to him in the first place. Moreover, Tobiah hardly got angry. Best of all, he often told her and others alike how beautiful and accommodating she was. Each day of their lives was as if they were newly married and exploring something new about the other. This night, Tobiah embraced his wife fondly, grateful to God that she did not apply any of the woman-made rules with regards to sexual intimacy that many of the new creature wives saddled themselves with.

CHAPTER 15

Let the Lord be magnified who takes pleasure in my prosperity.
Psalm 35:27

Levi was so excited to be at the Centre the following Friday evening. He needed to catch up on many things with Tim. Now that his family on both his father's and mother's sides were reunited, he felt lighter at heart. A kind of peace settled in his soul, and he felt free. Certainly, he was enjoying living the life of a new creature.

Mother Rachel had come to their home to help with the new infant. Two days later, his grandfather, Father Asher, and his entire family had come to visit! Many brethren had come visiting within the week, but the visit of Father Josef and his wife excited him the most. His mother's close friends had visited as well, with their husbands. And, for the first time, Timothy had come to visit with his family.

The Centre was packed, even more than usual, Levi thought. There were the usual testimonies, and his father went up to announce the arrival of the new arrival, Lemuel, who was just four days old. There was a wedding coming up between a sister Naomi and a brother Salmon. Then, before the fellowship ended with the prayer of Grace, Apostle Philip made an announcement that made his heart skip a beat or two.

'Dear brethren, these are times of uncertainty for the new creature. Because of our faith in Lord Jesus as the Messiah, incidences of persecution have begun to occur. Believers and their children are being molested. There have been two reported cases. Please be alert. I suggest our youths should always be in company with other youths their age or an adult – but never alone, please.

'Due to this, we have split Bethel Centre Fellowship into four other fellowship centres which will all meet on different days of the week. Please attend the one nearest your home to avoid attracting the attention of our enemies. Father Josef's house will accommodate fellowship for the Samuel Centre on Wednesdays. Father Asher's house will accommodate fellowship for the Dan Centre on Thursdays, the Bethel Centre will continue on Fridays, Father Nebo's house will accommodate fellowship for the Abel Centre on Saturdays and Father Lucas's house will accommodate fellowship for the Levi Centre on Sundays.'

Levi was stunned, and at that moment he and Timothy exchanged looks which spoke of their worry and distress at how things had suddenly turned for the worse for them both. Each saw tears in the other's eyes. Timothy nudged Levi to pay attention as Philip continued.

'This does not mean that as one fellowship we are being divided. Once a month, we will all come together to fellowship at each new centre in turn. The Apostles will preside each of these meetings. The evangelism outreach will start next week. Don't forget that just a little bit of light pushes away a lot of darkness, so four members from each centre will go out after their fellowship meeting for evangelism. A rota for this will be set out. The visitation team will be waiting after the service to meet with those who need home visits. Remember that showing kindness makes a difference.'

Levi looked round to see how others were affected by all these changes. The adults didn't seem so perturbed, but adults were like that. They put up a serene façade for the show, but often their minds thought differently. His eyes fell on Simeon the Junior, and they exchanged smiles. The service finished with the Grace, but fellowship continued as families, friends and newcomers exchanged greetings and gossip…

'Amaziah and Rebecca have settled well. I wonder which of our wealthy members gave them the house.'

'It is likely to be Sister Johanna.'

'I don't think so. Jephthah, her husband, loves money too much.'

'That may be true, but we saw him here today. Could he have had a change of heart?'

'I think it is the Lucas couple. They dined with them once.'

'Oh, did they? They dined with us two weeks ago, and we definitely have no spare houses to give out!'

'Oh!'

'Do you see Father Josef and Father Nebo talking over there?'

'Oh, yes. They must be pleased about their homes becoming centres. Nebo is doing very well as a stonemason, and—'

'Thank God for that. I remember that both of them used to be male prostitutes before they became new creatures.'

'Even Nebo too? We bless Abba! Yes! We even have reformed murderers here.'

'You don't say! Abba is merciful! Whom are you referring to?'

'Sister Naomi's betrothed is related to the family of Herod, who beheaded John the Baptist.'

'Ah, I get you now.'

'So, which of the centres will you be attending?'

'The Samuel Centre is nearer me.'

'Abba be praised. That is near me as well…'

'How did you like your first time at the Centre today?' Jonas asked.

'I was scared about the talk on all that stuff. Did it scare you, my brother?'

'Which one? About persecution or tribulation?' Jonas wanted to know.

'I wouldn't have understood all that! I must have dozed off. You know I merely attended since you promised you would mend my shoes for free.'

'Yes. Glad you came with me. Well, this was only my third time, but I wasn't scared. Which bit scared you?'

'That the day each person is born, their names and deeds are written in a book.'

'Oh yes, the Book of Life! What is scary about that, Abihu?'

'You and I are not new creatures, like the ones they talked about. We attend the synagogue where the Rabbi has rejected that Jesus was the Messiah. Did you not hear the Apostle say that because each new creature believes in Lord Jesus as their saviour, their names would not be blotted out from that book when they died?'

'I see what you mean,' Jonas confirmed.

'It was the clapping and shouts of joy that properly woke me up. I heard the Apostle clearly say that it was good to rejoice but that they should not forget their friends, relatives, and loved ones whose names will be blotted out from the Book of Life because they rejected the Messiah!' Abihu said.

'Yes, that is scary. There is no talk such as this in the synagogue. I want to continue coming and understand things better.'

'Me too, Jonas. But now that there are going to be new centres, won't they wonder who we are?'

'Let us go and see one of the Apostles and ask questions. One thing I certainly know is that everyone is welcome…'

'I can't believe Father did not keep our secret.' Leah said.

'My secret. Yet he promised. I am not going to ask him why, but I will not tell him any more secrets. I am sure he told Mother and a couple of his friends. Timothy says it is wrong to assume, though. What do you think, Leah? Should I confront our father or not?'

'You know, I don't know what to say. You have lived with our father longer than I. Can't you tell if he is trustworthy or not?'

'I am not sure. We only became close the week you joined the family.'

'Has he told you anything that has impressed you?' Leah asked.

'Yes, Leah. He has. You are quite right. I don't want to spoil the trust he has shown me. I won't confront him… but I feel betrayed, anyway.'

'Levi… what secrets did our father share with you?'

He smiled. 'Oh, just man stuff. Please don't ask me, because I don't want to tell you lies.'

Leah pouted. 'I promise not to tell anyone. Please?'

'No!'

'But you have told Timothy, haven't you?'

'No! Stop being nosey. Father might get to somehow know and won't trust me ever. Stop!'

'But—'

'Hey, children, what are you arguing about?' Their father was suddenly next to them, looking amused. 'So,' he continued when they remained silent, 'how have you enjoyed our service today without having to chase your brothers around?'

'Father, Mother Razi took them home with her family. Levi said it was fine,' said Leah.

Lucas grinned. 'Yeah, yeah, very fine. Shall we go home now?'

'Father, do you know the families that were harassed? You heard the Apostle, right?' Leah asked.

'Unbelievable, yes! That was what kept me a bit. I was listening to how Mother Ahuva's brother got molested – though it was the baker's son who was hit. Not by Romans, but fellow Jews who are not believers!'

'And I am sure there must be others not reported yet,' Leah added.

'Of course. Some people are being secretive so that others don't get unnecessarily scared.'

'But Father, that is wrong. Shouldn't every case be reported?'

'That wouldn't be wise. Breaking confidences is not godly. Right, Levi?'

'Right, Father.'

'You are unusually quiet.'

'I am still gutted with the fact that I may not be seeing Tim every Friday.'

'Why?' their father asked, looking shocked.

'We will each be stuck in different centres.'

'Not necessarily. We are not bound to one centre. People can attend the most convenient one. For example, people who have missed their own centre fellowship during the week because of their jobs or other issues can attend another centre. The new centres give people flexibility. Tim can attend whichever one he likes. I am not going to force either of you, but it is best for families to fellowship together. Right, Levi?'

'Right, Father.'

'Your secret is still safe with me, Levi.'

'And yours, too.'

'Very good, son, let's keep it that way.'

Leah smiled to herself on their way home. She knew how she was going to get the secret out of her brother.

'Thank you so much for introducing yourselves. Abba be praised. Is there something else you would like me to help you with?'

'We want to be new creatures, sir,' Abihu volunteered.

'You are both very welcome, Abihu the blacksmith and Jonas the shoemaker. It is the practice for believers to introduce themselves and share anything else God puts in their heart before the gathering; the church of Jesus Christ, like you must have seen today.'

'Yes,' they both replied.

'When a new believer is ready for this, they sit on the front benches.'

'Alright,' replied Jonas.

'As new believers, you need to both repeat a prayer after me. Are you both ready for this?'

'Yes,' they both said.

'Okay. Repeat after me…'

Abihu and Jonas repeated the prayer: *'Lord Jesus, I repent of all my sins. Please come into my heart and be my Lord and Saviour.'*

Apostle Philip embraced them in turn and asked them to kneel while he read from the book of Isaiah: *'No weapon forged against you will prevail, and you will refute every tongue that accuses you. This is the heritage of the servants of the Lord, and this is their vindication from Me, declares the Lord.'* He smiled at them. 'Now, please join any of the centres nearest to you, or this one if it is convenient.'

'By Heaven, tell me I am not dreaming, Yosey!'

'If I wasn't dreaming a moment ago about Jocheb, then you are not, my love. Who is it?'

'Take a discreet peek over your right shoulder. See that tall, mean looking man in that group? You can't miss him. The ruggedly handsome one in the purple shirt. His name is Lucas,' Ram whispered.

'Yes, yes, I see him now. What about him?'

'Many years ago, three men raped his sister in full view of some of us. Believe it or not, he took part in the rape himself, denying that she was his sister!' Ram stroked his beard.

'Are you sure? What an abomination! Many years is a long time, though,' Yosey exclaimed, shrugging his shoulders.

'Trust me, my love. I never forgot the woman or Lucas.'

'Ram, we are in business! New creatures in the skins of devils! Ha-ha-ha!' Yosey mocked. 'We will blackmail them. I can't wait!'

'Leave it all to me, Ram. I will make all the necessary enquiries. I very much want to avenge my pride that Jocheb abused four years ago,' Yosey said.

'I am hungry. Let us go and have a share of their meal,' Ram suggested.

'No! You dare not. It was such a meal that Jocheb ate, and he said it changed his affection towards me. That was how our affair ended.' He watched Ram laugh in disbelief.

'You surely don't believe such a lie, Yosey? You think a meal would change what we have between us? Come on, my love. We shall both partake of their meal, and you can shove his lies down his throat. Besides, Jesus is dead.'

'Don't take these things lightly, my love, please. I am not going to take the slightest chance. Have you not heard that the disciples of Jesus are doing miracles as well?' Yosey lowered his voice, a plea in his eyes.

'That is why we came here today. Did you see any?' Ram asked, not wanting to back down.

'No, but we cannot take our assumptions to the Sanhedrin, without proof that these people are traitors to our Jewish traditions. Please, we can always eat at *Safirah's Inn* on our way home.'

CHAPTER 16

*The thief comes only to steal and kill and destroy;
I have come that they may have life, and have it to the full.*
John 10:10

Thank you so much Abba, for this very beautiful bundle of joy You gave me six days ago. As Eliana searched baby Lemuel's face, drinking in every detail, she was sure he took after her. Like her first two children, he had a birthmark at the base of his back. She remembered with amusement the time both Levi and Leah had shown her their own birthmarks and how they had been truly amazed and very pleased when she showed them hers – their birthmarks were similar to hers and on the very same spot! Both children had been thrilled to learn that it was her birthmark which led to Mother Rachel finding her. The things Abba did! She found herself basking in the miracles in her life, and she could not resist relishing moments from her testimony.

Four years ago, I was twenty-seven-year-old Miriam, without parents, siblings, family, freedom, or salvation, but today… Abba, see, I am crying. It is all like a dream! You alone are the sole reason for my delight and happiness. Lord, to You I give my heart and my everything. I would never have guessed that by today I would be blessed with marriage, children, parents, and a big family.

She knew she was not yet close to her mother's side of the family, but over the year she had heard of two uncles her mother was in touch with, so perhaps she soon would be.

Today was going to be the first meeting in her home. Since it would be in the evening, there was plenty of time to prepare food and drinks for the guests. Many had seen Lemuel in the last three days, but many more would see him today. As soon as she heard the baby give a burp, she placed him back in his cot. It was just the third crow of dawn. It was early yet, but she would go and massage her tummy with hot water and belt it up with a strong cloth like she did with her other pregnancies after birth. She was determined to keep up her beautiful figure for as long as Abba would permit her life.

Apostle Philip was the first to arrive with his family, and Levi directed him to the part of their home allotted for the Levi Centre. He felt proud of their sanctuary, as his mother called it. Family prayers and school lessons took place here. It was here that his parents had revealed their past identities as old creatures to Leah and himself.

Soon the room was half full; Timothy's family and other familiar faces had turned up. Levi's mother could not sit still, and she walked around, rocking a little bundle in her arms. Soon his father called him to man the door to direct members. Shortly afterwards he saw two men whom he had never seen before, but that was not unusual. New members joined all the time. He assumed they were wealthy because they wore gold rings, and their clothes were of pure foreign linen.

'Is this the Levi Centre Fellowship?' one of them asked.

'Shalom,' Levi greeted. 'Yes. You are very welcome. Follow me.'

They didn't.

'Is this the house of Lucas?' The same man spoke. They wanted to be sure.

'You mean *Father Lucas*,' Levi stressed, puzzled by how they referred to his father.

At last, they followed him in. He heard them whisper between themselves, but it was inaudible. He didn't know that Yosey was whispering to Ram, 'Names have been changed!'

Soon Father Jephthah and his family were ushered in, with Razi and Josef following shortly afterwards.

'Hey, see who our gate man is! Master Levi!' Johanna said with a big smile. She exuded so much warmth, happiness, and love, it was infectious, and Levi caught it.

'Yes, the Honourable Master at your service. If you please, follow me. You are most welcome to the presence of the Most High!' They all laughed as he led them in. Inwardly, he was surprised to see them, considering their home would be hosting the Wednesday fellowship. So that was Mother Johanna's husband, he mused to himself. Then, just as he was about to join the main fellowship at the sound of the shofar, one more family sneaked in.

He was surprised how fast time went by and saddened that because of his duty at the door he had missed all the pre-fellowship time. He prayed that Tim would stay much longer afterwards.

As the fellowship wore on, Josef could hardly concentrate. He was tense and fidgety. His wife might even think his uneasiness was due to his past passion for Eliana. But the truth was that he had seen Yosey Uriah, his lover from a past life. Had he become a believer? How did he find this place? Who was the other man with him? What was his agenda? For revenge or to spy? They had been warned that there were spies sent by the Jewish elders seeking to destroy leaders and followers of the new faith introduced by Lord Jesus. Fourteen months ago, the fellowship had mourned for the gruesome murder of one of their leaders and prayed for God's comfort on his family, who were still regular members of the Bethel Fellowship. Soon, another new disciple had been apprehended and killed, and then all the Lord's Apostles and all the new creatures had to be even more careful. Some even changed their names.

During the welcome and greetings after the time of praise and worship, he would go and greet Yosey. He decided to warn Razi first. He blessed Abba in his heart that he and his wife had opened up about their pasts. 'My beloved, please listen without a stir,' he whispered slowly and very quietly with a smile. Observers might have thought he was just chatting about Apostle Philip's sermon or maybe about something in the family.

Razi nodded.

'Yosey, from my past, is here,' he said to her.

She nodded again, but this time she squeezed his hands, gently whispering, 'Abba has your back.'

During the welcome and greetings session, Levi saw lots of people going to see baby Lemuel. Tim said to him, 'is that a new employee talking to your father by the door?'

'I don't know. He is new here, because he addressed my father without a title.'

'Really? He may not be a Jew. God has sent him here for deliverance.' Then after a pause, 'Levi, have you told Leah not to listen to your friend Jesse?' Tim asked rather anxiously.

'Obviously not. She is talking to him right now. You talk to Jesse yourself. I don't have to come with you. Go on, Tim! Be bold. Jesse doesn't even know that Leah is only ten!'

As Tim left, Levi looked for Father Josef. He wanted to greet him but could not find him anywhere. *That's strange. Maybe Mother Razi will explain.*

As he made his way towards her, Tim's mother approached him. 'Levi, has Tim told you the good news yet?'

'What good news?'

'Ah well, it will soon be announced. Tim will have a new father and siblings!'

'*Mazel tov*, Mother Adah! You too will get a new husband!'

'Abba be praised. Where is Tim? I thought you were inseparable when together.'

Soon the shofar sounded as people returned to their seats. Levi noticed that both his father and Father Josef did not return to their seats. *That's strange.* His baby brother must have awoken, because his mother had gone to the very back of the room where other mothers sat to nurse their infants.

The rest of the service ran the way it usually did at the Bethel Centre. During the announcements at the end was the reminder that the following Friday would be the Passover, and a lot of visitors and Jews from all over Judea would come to Jerusalem to observe the feast as Moses had commanded.

'Lemuel, you have brought me so much good fortune today,' Eliana murmured to her son as she thought about the day. It had been so wonderful to see Lucas bonding with Jephthah and Josef, particularly when Josef had come to see the baby. At the time, her mother was holding Lemuel, and she was free to greet brethren. Josef had merely hugged her, like other men had done, but she had been excited at his touch. It brought forbidden memories and aroused sexual images of them both. 'Jocheb' was the only man in those times who made love to her as a man would with a woman and not a prostitute. It was with him she had remembered being Dinah and had begun to yearn for the true love between a husband and a wife. He was much better looking and stronger than her own husband, and she discerned her husband was secretly envious. She hoped she had kept a look of innocence, but she wondered if she had expressed too much joy and surprise when he had come over. Maybe, with time, they would get used to being around each other. Josef said that they had decided to seize the opportunity to see Lemuel and offer her and Lucas their good wishes. *Ah, Josef, Josef. It was good to see you again. We are both in the same evangelism team. If I am wise, I should join a different team...*

Lucas saw the same Sunday evening in a different light, as his mind kept mulling over the moment he had set eyes on Ram and his unknown companion, both of whom had promptly disappeared after making threats of blackmail. They had threatened to announce Lucas's involvement in his sister's rape at the next gathering! Ram had called him a pervert, amongst other things. 'Look, Lucas, you want to save your honour, name, and pride, right? Just give me what I ask. Your wife is very rich. Give me ownership of your property in Sidon. Come with the signed document that relinquishes the property to me,' he had said before leaving with the stranger.

Lucas was thoroughly confused. What would happen if he gave in to releasing the property the following Friday when Ram would come to collect the agreed documents? His spirit was low, yet he had to keep up a serene and calm disposition. Would it be better to confide in his wife? That would give her the edge over him in terms of sins committed in their pasts. Right now, he was enjoying her complete obligation to keep him happy, satisfied and fulfilled in their marriage. She was Dinah in bed and had continued to refer to him as *'my lord'*, the way she had when she was Dinah. How would this information about his past affect the way things were between them right now? He could not tell. She had given him total authority to handle her wealth and property as he saw fit. Would she be offended that he had not completely revealed his entire past? She herself was not willing to divulge the names of those she had slept with. He knew she had lied about sleeping with the husbands of some of her friends when she was a prostitute. Why could she not trust him? It hurt him, and he knew that he would always feel betrayed and insecure whenever he saw any man. Take, for example, the way he felt when he saw Josef hug her. It seemed that something invisible had transpired between them, and he had felt so jealous. He needed that reassurance of her confiding totally in him. If he approached her about what she now felt for Josef, she would become defensive and refer to the promise he had made never to bring up her past relationships to hurt her.

It was therefore not an option to approach her about her past relationships or the threat from Ram. It was a dilemma. Whom could he talk to? If he spoke to an Apostle, would he be asked to testify, or would it be kept in confidence? He wasn't sure. He might speak to Father Asher, as Plan A. He had wisdom, and Lucas secretly admired the way he ran his home in full and fair control of his family. He decided to attend the fellowship in his house on Thursday. For Plan B, he might succumb to giving up the property at Sidon.

But there was one thing that bothered him the most. Blackmailing never ended once it begun…

The rest of Sunday had also been different for Razi and Josef. Josef had assured Razi that all was well. He told her that when he greeted Eliana she felt like a sister; he had not felt anything from his old nature with her. But that was not what Razi was worried about.

'Yes, my beloved,' she said, 'I am sure of that. I meant Yosey. What did he want?'

'Oh, he heard I still run my boating company and wanted to know if I could take on his nephew as an apprentice.'

'You were gone for quite a while, my beloved.'

'I know, my love. I was so curious; I wanted to know how he knew where I lived, how he became a new creature, and I just wanted to catch up on people we both knew. We even planned to meet up on Saturday to see if we could invite some people to the Centre next Sunday.'

'How wonderful, my beloved. That is evangelism. Although Yosey has not been presented to the Apostles or the fellowship – he needs to before joining the evangelism team.'

'You are right. I will go early in the morning to see Apostle Jude. He is in charge of evangelism. I will ask his advice. I do not want to quench the budding zeal of Yosef…'

Josef knew he had succeeded in fooling his wife – but not God. He was torn about telling his wife the truth. If he told her that he had been blackmailed, she would worry herself so much she might possibly miscarry. He was not going to take that risk on her delicate health. He was going to fix the problem himself.

And Eliana? A shower of calm descended upon his low mood and raised it up several notches. *Miriam.* He knew he was deceiving himself. He realised the moment he saw her that he had to make a choice about how to respond to her. He struggled for the first few seconds as his mind conjured up her nude image; she definitely gave him a 'Miriam' look rather than an Eliana one. He still felt infatuated by her and knew he would be wise to steer far away from her. He knew that if they were alone, he would desire to kiss her.

He was also aware that he was consciously submerging his fear of Yosey Uriah. Had he been wise in their encounter today? Could he have done things differently?

'Jocheb, you betrayed me and lied to me! You never once mentioned that you had the love of a woman on the side. Why? Why? That was the basis for which I paid you handsomely?'

Josef had paused for a moment. 'I am happy to compensate. How much should I pay you?'

'It is not a question of money. You totally abandoned me and left me to wallow in the pit of depression and frustration. You used the excuse of the bread of Jesus that you ate.'

'That was true, though.'

'I don't care about all that now! I am after revenge. I am ready to stand up before your so-called new creatures and tell them that we were lovers, and—'

'Please don't do that,' Josef interrupted. *'I have asked how I can compensate you for the past. I am now a new creature, and—'*

Yosey cut in. *'All I am asking is that you visit me… and give me one last time with Jocheb. Then all my pain and bitterness against you will disappear.'*

'How about your present partner? You know that won't be fair.'

'Jocheb, do we have a deal or not?'

Josef had panicked. 'We do.'

'See you on Saturday, mid-morning, my darling. If you don't come, then you will see me on Sunday standing before the congregation to tell everyone. Think about what that will do to your wife and family members who never knew!'

Josef sighed as he thought back over the conversation. There didn't seem a way out at the time, and there wasn't one now. He could not tell Razi. Who could he talk to?

I can speak to Father Benjamin. He knows Razi very well. It was him who brought us together. I cannot give in to Yosey's demand. There will be further blackmail... and who knows what next?

CHAPTER 17

*I have hidden your word in my heart
that I might not sin against you.*
Psalm 119:11

Eliana marvelled at how quickly the week had gone by. She was glad that her husband had asked Leah to man the door this Sunday, and Levi had been granted the privilege to enjoy the Thursday fellowship at his grandparents' home so he could be with Tim. This Sunday, she sat and enjoyed the entire service because her mother minded the baby, who slept straight through for two hours. She savoured every bit of the service. They shared bread and wine in memory of their being saved from the plagues of Egypt and their freedom from slavery. During the Passover message, Apostle Jude reminded brethren to remember that the devil was looking for people to devour; to take their freedom and make them slaves to sin. As new creatures, they were all vulnerable. Their hearts were clean, emptied of all the past sins and filth which Abba had taken away by the death and crucifixion of Jesus. They were to remember that demons were around, looking for a new abode. From time to time, those demons would return to see if their hearts were receptive. Passover was a time to remember all that Jesus had done for them, and their hearts should be made ready and clean to eat the bread.

The room was full, and there were some new faces as usual. Eliana had heard that this was the case in many centres, despite the persecutions going on after the death of Lord Jesus. Many who were once Zealots, Pharisees, Sadducees, members of the Sanhedrin and even Romans were seeking to become new creatures!

Josef and his family were not there; she felt relieved at that.

Something Apostle Jude said registered in her spirit: 'Resist the devil and he will flee from you. Do not expect to see an ugly horned beast appear to you and tempt you. He will come in various ways, such as when people open their hearts to lies, deception, unforgiveness, pride, hatred, vengeance, murder, blackmail, slander, lust in their hearts, and secret sins. Remember that your victory and honour come from the Lord alone. He is your Refuge and Rock where no enemy can reach you if you remain free from sin. Always pray for help, and angels will be sent to help you instantly.'

She made up her mind there and then that she would not be in the same team as Josef. She also prayed to Abba that whenever she and Josef were together, she would be strengthened from above.

The day before had been spectacular, and her recollections of it momentarily snatched her attention away from Apostle Jude. Lucas had said he was going to pay a visit to Father Asher to keep up their good relationship but particularly so they could discuss business. Her mother had gone with him, taking the opportunity to visit her home. When they returned much later in the evening, Lucas had looked sober, his usually upbeat disposition soured. Maybe he was just tired. Her mother did not say anything was amiss. Still, she had discerned a burden weighing his mind down.

She glanced at her husband now. His rapt attention to the Apostle stirred her thoughts back to fellowship.

Lucas was far from being attentive inwardly, though, even though outwardly he seemed mesmerised by the message. His choice of Father Asher as the right confidant had been perfect. Father Asher had abandoned his wife when she desperately needed his help. To make matters worse, he had given away or sold their ailing baby daughter. He would understand. Lucas had not found it difficult to tell him how he had treated his sister in his old nature, but Father Asher had looked at the whole matter from a different angle Lucas had not considered. Two heads were surely better than one, he thought as he reflected on their conversation:

'Don't crucify yourself, Lucas! You did not kill the saints of Christ, as Apostle Paul did. Yet Paul assumed he was doing it for God. That was your own standing too when you joined supporters of Jesus to attack your sister, whom you saw as aligning with our enemy.'

'I can understand that, Father Asher, but how does that get me out of having to sign off one of Eliana's properties to this blackmailer?'

'Yes, you got that right. A blackmailer. They thrive on secrecy. Lucas, it's all a bluff. Sit calmly tomorrow at the service. When he calls you to go out with him, tell him to wait till the end. Whatever way it turns out, do not go alone. Go with Eliana and any of the Apostles.'

'But I do not want anyone else to know.'

'I know that, but there is nothing that is hidden from the sun. Did I ever imagine that my own sin would find me out? Lucas, get it off your chest, and tell Eliana the truth. You are both new creatures, and all will be well.'

'Won't she think I have more skeletons in my cupboard?'

'Do you?'

'*No, but she has. She has refused to divulge the names of clients she slept with. I am sure you understand how this might affect me.*'

'*I do... and so would every man who is not married to a virgin. I find it a mystery that you took my prostitute daughter as your wife, but then I remember that so did Salmon with Rahab, the prostitute of Jericho, or Boaz with Ruth, the Moabite woman! My advice is that you make a pact with her. She tells you what you want to know, and you tell her your story.*'

'*It sounds simple, but I fear it isn't,*' Lucas said, recalling his wife's stories of the bad and good parts of her life.

'*Then what else do you fear? You said that your sister and husband have forgiven you.*'

'*Yes. That is another miracle.*'

'*Indeed. We can pray for Abba, the God of miracles, to turn things round to your favour – starting with your wife and extending to your blackmailing acquaintance. Abba is the God of Abraham and Jacob – who weren't perfect. No one is perfect. I am not. Yet Abba has overlooked my imperfections and exalted me. He will do the same for you. I am not a praying person, but Mother Rachel prays for everything, every situation. Trust me. Abba has always listened. She does not need to know the details. Let her tell Abba to give you successful business with a former acquaintance. That should do. Good thing she is home.*'

'*Thank you, Father Asher. Please ask her to pray.*'

Lucas had felt very confident, encouraged, and hopeful after Mother Rachel's prayers. He looked at Ram now. Mother Rachel had prayed for Abba's blessings to fall on him! They had avoided each other when the brethren went around greeting one another. Ram had come stealthily into the fellowship, made straight for Lucas and demanded the documents. But Lucas had told him to wait till the end of service so that he did not draw attention to himself or give cause for his wife to wonder. Ram had agreed. Lucas had thanked God for that favour. Things were going well so far. He could not wait for the service to be over. Ram was in for a shock.

'You are already up and dressed, my beloved,' Razi said to her husband in surprise.

'Sorry, my love. I tried to be as quiet as possible.'

'It's fine. I didn't realise you meant to visit Apostle Jude this early. He might not be awake yet.'

Josef shrugged. 'Well, that is what he signed up for, being an Apostle. I must be on my way now.'

'Let us pray briefly, my beloved.'

'Really brief, then.'

'Abba, please send your angels ahead of Josef to touch the hearts of all whom he will meet today. May his words bring him favour and success, to Your own glory, in Jesus Christ's name we ask. Amen.'

'Amen,' he said, planting a kiss on her head and then her belly as she lay back on the bed.

On the way to Father Benjamin's house, he decided to call first at Yosey's home. A lot of people were already up, going about their various business. Goatherds, shepherds, sellers of milk, cheese, bread, and other goods, traders and even men with horses and carts waiting to carry passengers. He decided against using a horse as it might attract unwanted attention, being a way of announcing status.

After a little over twenty-five minutes' walk, he arrived at Yosey's. He tapped the door in the way that Yosey would recognise, then tapped louder two more times, and soon he heard movement within. 'See who is here before the scheduled time,' Yosey greeted him, his eyes sparkling.

'Is this a bad time?' Josef asked very quietly, with no intention to go inside.

'No, no,' Yosey whispered with excitement. 'Come in, my darling. I am alone, and I was just—'

'I actually came to ask for your pardon and to plead that you forget everything. Please, Yosey.'

Yosey frowned. 'Are we going back on our word? Make haste. I will be waiting for you.'

Josef didn't turn away but let some seconds lapse before speaking. 'Please, Yosey.'

Yosey shook his head. 'I'm sorry, but you did not show *me* such kindness back then.'

Josef felt hope escaping him. He had thought Razi's prayers would sort things out. 'Yosey... please reconsider accepting money. I'm not like that anymore. Besides—'

'I have said *no*. Can you come in? Passers-by might think I am in some sort of trouble.'

'Not now. I must go and create my alibi, or my wife will catch me out. I will return at the agreed time or just a little later. Before I go... Yosey, please forgive me.'

'I will be waiting for you, as agreed.'

The door was shut firmly in Josef's face.

He felt agitated. Something strange had happened. He had felt the old desire, his body lusting for forbidden love with Yosey. *'Abba, please don't forget our prayers. Please work in his heart when I return. Or do You want me to sin against you? Please, Abba. I need your help,'* he prayed out openly, sighing.

He was not willing to walk the forty minutes to the east side of Jerusalem. There were more people about now, he thought; he would not be the only horse rider. He hired a horse, and, within fifteen minutes, he was at Father Benjamin's abode. He jumped off, tied the horse to a suitable post and walked slowly to the door, soaking in the early morning sun's rays.

Father Benjamin was surprised to hear his fifteen-year-old grandson, Moses, say that Father Josef was waiting in their living room. It surprised him because they were not on any outreach teams together. He hoped all was well.

'Good morning, Father Benjamin. Shalom.' Josef rose to greet the elder respectfully as he came in.

'Good morning, son. Shalom. How are Razi and Samuel?'

'They are fine.'

'Do you want to join me for breakfast in the kitchen?' Father Benjamin asked, remaining standing.

'No, thank you. Please finish your breakfast. I can wait.'

'I insist.'

Josef was glad for the breakfast, as he hadn't realised how hungry he was. Mother Tamara's food was delicious.

'So... how can we help you?' Father Benjamin said as they finished their food. 'You didn't just come all the way to say hello.' Both men laughed.

As they left the dining area, Josef whispered, 'Take me somewhere very private, where you are sure there will be no eavesdroppers.'

'Eavesdroppers? Not a chance in this household. Eavesdropping is a sign of lacking trust or a sense of insecurity. Some folk depend on eavesdropping to ensure that the world as they see it is the same. Well, let me not divert your purpose this morning. Follow me to my prayer room. Not even Mother Tamara will seek to come in when we are there.'

'Thank you, Father Benjamin.'

'Tamara!' He called out. 'I am in the prayer room.'

'I hear you, my husband,' she replied quietly.

The men sat down. 'So, Josef, how are you and the family doing? Judging from seeing you every week, I am sure things are fine with you.'

'Yes. That is true. But someone from my past wants to destroy my family, my reputation, and my happiness. That is why I am here.'

'Josef, you do not even have to tell me any details. Abba already knows.'

'But… if I don't tell you, how will you know what to pray for?'

Benjamin leant forward and placed his hand on Josef's. 'Don't worry, my son. Let us pray: *Abba, thank you that we do not have to worry about anything because we can pray and ask for your help on anything. Right now, we ask for your divine intervention concerning whatever issue Josef is facing that brought him here. We thank You because You have it all sorted out – whatever it is that Josef needs. Give him Your wisdom and peace; we ask in Jesus Christ's name, Amen.*'

'Amen,' Josef concurred without conviction.

'And that is it. You can go in peace.'

Josef felt disappointed. 'Thanks, Father Benjamin… but I needed advice on a very pressing issue.'

'Whose advice would you take? Mine or Abba's?'

'Abba's.'

'Good. So be it. Abba is omnipotent, omnipresent, omniscient, and omnibenevolent. Trust Him. My advice is that you go straight home and rejoice for the victory Abba has given you.'

Josef did as he advised. Let Abba's will be done! He would attend to his business on Sunday and attend the Samuel fellowship scheduled in his own home on Wednesday.

'*What does Abba have in His plans for me?*' Eliana asked herself again and again. Just the day before, her husband had stripped her soul naked and she felt raw, sore, and still bleeding and in pain. The shame of prostitution had never quite left; it had been adorned on her head, and her husband revealing his own dark secret involving his sister did not make her feel better. He had thought he had a 'just' cause for his actions back then. Maybe he too felt pain anytime he saw his sister and her family. All she knew right now was that she felt stripped of all the dignity and pride she had. Worse, she began to feel that everyone could see the 'cap of prostitution' on her head.

When she wrested her mind back to the fellowship, the Apostle was blessing the congregation. Then came the announcements, the last of which caught her attention: '…You have been fearful; you have been questioning your faith or even doubting Abba's love for you. Please come forward and take hold of the promises of Abba over your life. The Word of God is that you should be at peace with the truth of who Jesus Christ is for you as a new creature. No more condemnation. It is the devil trying to steal your peace. I repeat: if you need to feel this peace within yourself, step forward in faith. Don't hold back now or listen to the devil keeping you seated. Come out and let the Holy Spirit wash over your soul, mind, and body.

From her seat at the back, Eliana saw a number of people respond to the Apostle's request. Very much encouraged, she rose with her head bowed down and went forward.

'May the power of the Holy Spirit of Abba descend on you all and grant His favour upon you, your family, your children, and a thousand generations and more. May His presence go before you, around you, in your coming and going from this moment. May you all experience the peace that came upon you when you first heard about or were touched by Lord Jesus. For those of you coming here for the first time or still in your old nature, may Abba visit you with His salvation, that you may turn from your sinful ways.

'Peace He leaves with you; his peace He gives you – not as the world gives. So do not let your hearts be troubled, nor be fearful. As new creatures, you will enjoy eternity with Abba at the end of your time. May the God of hope fill you all with joy and peace. I ask all this in the name of Jesus Christ, Amen.'

'Amen,' everyone chorused loudly together with hearty claps.

It was time for the usual end of fellowship activities. Brethren shared cake-bread and wine as they greeted one another or gossiped. Eliana felt the peace and love of Abba suffuse all over her being. The pain and raw feelings of shame, hurt, and low self-esteem had been replaced by Christ's righteousness that made her a new creature. Why had she given way to the devil, allowing him to steal her joy and peace? She was a daughter of the most High God, who saw her as righteous! Why should she not hold her head proudly and bask in His love? If Lucas wanted to know every sordid detail of her life as a prostitute, why not? If she was going to share her infectious testimony with other prostitutes, she needed to sound confident, convincing… and even cheerful.

Lucas looked out for Ram and his friend, but they were nowhere to be seen. As he searched the thinning crowd, he saw his brother-in-law, Father Amaziah. 'Good to see you again,' he greeted genuinely.

'Good to see you too, Lucas.'

There was no sense of his past guilt. Abba had taken care of it. Why had he allowed himself to wallow in terror that Abba would fail him? He saw Eliana. She looked less tense, and her joy amongst the brethren was sincere. He would surprise her with the news of his intention to visit Jephthah during the week and take over her business from him.

Yosey did not feel sorry for himself that Jocheb had not turned up. It did not surprise him, considering what he had just heard Apostle Jude say: *'When temptation comes, flee',* or something like that. What irked him was everyone pretending not to know who Jocheb was whenever he asked them. He was sure they knew his old name. He decided to ask the Apostle himself – an Apostle would not pretend but would tell the truth.

'Good sir, can you kindly tell me how I could locate a man who used to go by the name of Jocheb, but now has a new name? In fact, he was here last Sunday.'

'Do you know his second name or the new name?'

'I can't remember.'

'Or anything about his wife, family, or his looks that could help?'

'He is extremely tall and very good looking.'

Instantly, Apostle Jude knew who he meant, but said, 'Oh, is it Father Isaiah over there?' They had been warned to be cautious in giving details to strangers who masked themselves as innocent; like wolves in sheep's clothing.

'No,' Yosey said, 'he is not here. I have already asked around.'

'Is it something I may be able to help you with?'

'Not really. I will be here next Sunday.'

'Alright, but please wait. I feel the need to pray for you.'

Out of courtesy, Yosey tolerated the request; after all, he had been impressed and touched by the message. Part of him yearned to enjoy the privileges and benefits of these 'new creatures'. He needed that peace. As Jude laid his hands on him, he felt shaky all the way down to his feet. He felt a sensation of possession over his body, which he tried hard to resist but could not. He felt himself sinking…

Ram anxiously wondered what was taking his lover so long. He took himself back to the main room, where he was lucky to still find some bread and wine which he gladly took to abate his mounting hunger. What had Yosey said would happen if one ate this meal? He still felt the same. Then he saw Lucas and a woman. That was the woman – Rebecca! His sister! They were obviously new creatures. She had forgiven her brother – how? Lucas was soon joined by a very beautiful woman who placed a new infant in his arms. Then Ram saw Rebecca's husband wrap his arms around her waist. Why had Lucas seemed so scared?

They were all truly happy, content, at peace with their families, and blessed. Could he, Ram, or many others he knew, say the same for themselves?

Jude's message had touched his heart, and he no longer wanted to be a slave of sin. All the same, it would be a bonus if Lucas fell for the blackmail. Having a property to himself for nothing? He could not let that opportunity slip by. He meandered his way amongst brethren towards Lucas at the other side of the large room.

'Shalom,' he greeted Lucas and those around him as he approached them.

'Shalom, Ram!' Lucas burst out. 'Rebecca, this is a miracle. Ram was a witness to that ugly scene, and he has not forgotten!'

Rebecca smiled softly. 'Ram, God is so good. Don't ever hate yourself. I was two months pregnant when you all raped me, but God protected my unborn child, and—'

'I was not a participator, just an onlooker, but—'

'Yes,' Rebecca cut in, 'I have forgiven Lucas and all the others. Abba has been merciful. He has blessed me and reunited me to my family. Are you a new creature now?'

All eyes were on him, and he suddenly felt awkward. To say no meant they might think him a spy. 'Yes,' he said, but before he could move away, he was surrounded by rejoicing brethren who embraced him and took him to the Apostle. He was stunned that everything was happening so fast.

A little later, he saw a red-eyed Yosey, who drew him to one side. 'I have confessed my sins, Ram,' he whispered. 'I am now a new creature.'

'I know. Me too... but how are we going to report back to those who sent us? We would be killed as traitors.'

'Come. Follow me,' Yosey said, leading Ram to an empty bench. 'Sit here, my friend, and wait for me.'

Ram watched in amazement as Yosey spoke to some brethren with familiarity, then came back with them following him. 'Ram,' one of the brethren said, 'we would like you and Yosey to listen to the testimony of a brother you both know well. Please remain here for five minutes while we fetch him. You both need to hear him.'

'Father Lucas,' called another, 'please take your horse and fetch Father Nicodemus.'

'*Nicodemus!*' Ram whispered in disbelief as he exchanged glances with an equally surprised Yosey.

As Lucas rushed out to fetch Nicodemus, he praised Abba. *'Thank you, Abba! Seth is Amaziah's, not mine. You have freed me indeed...'*

CHAPTER 18

Believers will be given the power to perform miracles:
they will drive out demons in my name;
they will speak in strange tongues;
if they pick up snakes or drink poison,
they will not be harmed;
they will place their hands on sick people who will get well.
Mark 16:17-18

Many ladies of red had been told that Miriam, who was formerly known as a prostitute in all of Jerusalem but currently known as Eliana, wanted to speak to them and offer them gifts. She was coming with some fellow ex-prostitutes. A date had been given and word had gone round. Many of them had heard of the very wealthy woman who owned the famous *Miriam's House of Pleasures* and other pleasure houses in Judea. Many came out of curiosity. Many had heard that she had changed her lifestyle. Some wanted to know how they could be saved from their own lives of prostitution. Some knew she was living a new life and wanted to see for themselves that she was free from the demons of lust, oppression, and sexual addiction. Others came hoping to learn tricks and be materially blessed. Still others came because they believed this could be an invitation for them to be reformed. Some came because they were without hope, and anything offered as a way out of their hopelessness was welcome. They all knew that she was once a prostitute, and she was coming with others who had also been prostitutes. What had changed – and how?

Eliana, Razi, Biliah, and Johanna prayed fervently, asking God to keep them safe from any harm. They asked Abba to send His angels to ward off the Romans, Zealots, Pharisees and all who persecuted followers of Lord Jesus. They asked Abba to touch the hearts of many prostitutes and unbelievers with the new teachings of Lord Jesus so that they would be blessed. Sister Naomi prayed the favour of Abba upon them; that His miraculous power would fall on all who would attend. She prayed that Abba would give Eliana and her evangelism team the wisdom, strength, and courage to speak boldly without shame or fear.

Over a hundred angels were dispatched instantly; some to Eliana and her crew and others to the gathering of women at the west gates of Jerusalem, where *Miriam's House of Pleasures* – Eliana's former residence – was.

Leah was impressed with the way her mother and her friends had organised the evangelistic meeting. She felt proud of the women and wondered at that moment how her brother Levi must be feeling. He was going to hear once again their father openly divulge the secrets of his past to a gathering of other men. At least Levi was in the company of his closest friends – Tim, Moses, and a few others. She wished she also had a very close friend who could pass as a sister. She looked at Jana, sitting beside her, who was fourteen and not much of a companion. She wondered why. She was Moses's sister, but they were so different.

Leah shifted her attention back to her mother, who was richly dressed and did not seem too anxious. Everyone had been treated to a sumptuous feast, and she was sure they were delighted to hear that they were going to be further treated to songs from each of their hosts. This was fun! She was glad that she had come. She remembered how surprised and pleased she had felt when her request to participate had been granted. She hoped her twin brothers would fall asleep so that Mother Rachel could enjoy what she was enjoying.

Eliana was the first to sing. The sight of her ex-colleagues, still wallowing in ignorance and darkness and blind to the love, salvation, and deliverance of Lord Jesus, touched her deeply. She understood at that point how Lord Jesus was always moved to compassion because He saw humans as people without true sight; people who helplessly fell into all manner of pits.

She remembered how she had felt all those years ago when there was no other way of survival for her but prostitution. There had been no family, or friends, or hope. She had felt she had no future and had lived for what the present day brought. Yet the path to salvation and deliverance had come knocking on her door through friends like Josef, Johanna, and Razi. She remembered her doubts, fear, and insecurity – can it ever happen to me? Can this life ever change? Will Lord Jesus give me all that I yearn for in my heart? Can I ever live a normal life and be accepted by society? She thought about when she had met Lord Jesus and how He had transformed her. He was gone now, but He left something in them all to share with others. And she was ready.

Eliana imagined that the assorted faces before her were masking their thoughts and the doubts rolling through their minds. She prayed to Abba that the song she was about to render would touch them, that every shred of doubt and every ounce of worry would be dispelled as they listened to her sing and then share her own testimony.

Leah watched her mother. She was silent, as if wrestling in her mind about which song to sing. Or was she suddenly seized with anxiety or regret or shame? Why was she standing there looking at each face? Leah was relieved when she heard her mother pray a prayer as if it was a song, but she felt a little disappointed at first because she was expecting a solo rendering of a proper song.

'Abba Father, Abba God, Abba my rescuer, Abba my helper, Abba… You are my real love. I have tasted You, and You are so, so sweet. You have touched *me,* and You are a miracle. You saw my hard, cold, empty, and dead heart and You made it soft, made it warm, filled it with You – and now I live in You.

There is darkness here, Abba; there is pain here, Abba; there is doubt here, Abba. Abba, my deliverer, show Yourself here. Let there be light; let there be light; let there be light.'

Eliana allowed silence to fall for a few moments, then said, 'I am going to sing a song I have specially chosen for this day. When you hear my testimony in a few minutes, you will understand why this song ministers to me so much. It is a song deposited in my soul from Abba. Listen, and be blessed.'

Leah felt better. Things were going as expected. Her mother's sweet, slow, almost hypnotic voice captivated her, and tears welled in her eyes as she listened to this marvellous woman who had become her mother about fifteen months ago.

> *'Things are different now.*
> *Something happened to me*
> *when I gave my life to Jesus.*
> *Things I loved before*
> *have passed away.*
> *Things I never loved have come to stay.*
> *Things are different now.*
> *Something happened to me*
> *when I gave my life to Jesus.'*

The angel of praise had put the song in Eliana's heart, and it blessed her audience. They wept. They wanted to be blessed like she was. They wanted the freedom. They wanted to be accepted.

They wanted the love and salvation Abba had offered Eliana and was offering them even now as they heard her sing.

'Why do I rejoice, you ask?' Eliana said into the hushed silence. 'What did Abba do for me? How did Abba transform me? You want to know. I will tell you.

'I was about three months old. Ill. No hope of survival. My two brothers were killed in one day, as commanded by King Herod, and my mother became mentally ill. My father, who could not cope, sold me to Gwabar – the child abductor over there.' She pointed and Leah saw a man stand up and give a wave to the gathered guests in the room. Some gave a surprised gasp. Leah was horrified and felt shocked at hearing her mother's life story in such detail.

'I was exploited from the age of four and made to believe I was an orphan. At eight, prostitution started and lasted for twenty-one years, till I was twenty-nine. At eighteen, I got married and had two children I had to abandon as babies because their father discovered I was a prostitute. You can all imagine my thoughts as this unfortunate orphan: no siblings, no family, no husband – and no hope of ever seeing the children I brought into the world or of knowing their welfare. I built up my wealth here in Jerusalem, in this very house, with no joy or peace of mind. That was until I learnt of Lord Jesus through a client, Josef, and fellow prostitutes who had been reformed but did not abandon or forget me: Biliah, Johanna, and Razilla. They proved their love for me by taking me to meet Him!'

Leah found herself clapping with zeal along with others at these wonderful friends of her mother.

'Miracles started happening to me which you will never believe! Abba led me to my birth parents, my husband, my family, my children, and a new life as a new creature!'

Eliana saw people rejoice for her as if what they heard was beyond their understanding and imagination. She would not be surprised if the women here today thought they had just been told a fairy tale. She too was still in awe of all Abba had done for her since she had put her faith in the gospel of Lord Jesus.

After briefly explaining how some of the events happened, she introduced her mother and Leah and let her guests know that her husband, along with the husbands of her friends, was also at that moment conducting a similar outreach to the men of Sidon.

'Before I take my seat, I want you to know that Lord Jesus rose from the dead after He was crucified because He is the Messiah sent by God to free us all from slavery to sin.'

A heavy silence followed.

'Because Lord Jesus lives, I have no fears. I can always trust that Abba is always looking out for me, blessing me, and answering my prayers. This is what we want you all to enjoy. Thank you.'

Leah clapped. The speech had been moving, convincing and very touching. During her introduction, she heard lots of people say she looked like her mother, and she felt proud.

Mother Razi came out next; attractive but not as breath-taking as her mother or eye-catching as Mother Johanna, yet she had been blessed by the most handsome and wonderful husband – Father Josef. She looked tired, and her waist was quite thick, but her face radiated trust, confidence, and inner strength. Leah could not wait for the singing. She wanted to know whose song would be the best and whose voice was the sweetest with the most impact. She drew her attention back to Mother Razi.

'My song will express how I feel – how a woman like me started life as a young girl full of dreams and hopes. I had loving parents who were slaves, but they sheltered me and promised to always be there for me. My dreams all crashed when I was separated from them at the age of eleven. I had no other family, no hope of ever living a different life other than prostitution. I had no hope of getting married or having children, since I was an outcast. For ten terrible years, I was in this hopeless pit; fearing each day. My spirit rejected prostitution, yet what could I have done? I did not know Lord Jesus, and I was a Gentile. Abba sent Father Simeon to meet with me in a hotel in Sidon. He led me to Lord Jesus, and I am now a new creature enjoying the fellowship of brethren and freedom from sin. I now have my peace, my joy, and the love of Lord Jesus all over me. I have a husband, two sons, and I am expecting a third miracle,' she said shyly to loud cheers. 'I couldn't keep Lord Jesus all to myself, and that is why I told my friends, and I am telling you all now. Believe on Lord Jesus and He will save you too. Listen to my song, and be blessed by Abba:

'When I think of the goodness of Jesus
and all He has done for me,
my soul cries out, 'Alleluia' –
Praise God for saving me!'

Mother Razi was dramatic. Her voice and song really conveyed her warmth, joy, peace, and love for Abba. She stunned everyone with the beauty of her singing. Leah grudgingly had to accept that Mother Razi's singing had more impact on her, and she felt it was the same for other listeners. It was the way she shook her head, waved her hands, opened or shut her eyes, uttered melodic sounds or moved her body at the right moments to synchronise with the meaning of what she was singing. The overall effect heightened the impact, and she received a standing ovation with cheerful clapping and hoots of praise. Leah asked herself how that reaction from the guests was possible since her mother had experienced more miraculous incidents. Most of the audience were crying and saying, 'Give me Jesus; show me how to get Jesus; I want to be saved; I believe Lord Jesus can save me too...'

Razi waited.

What was she going to say after calm was regained? Leah wondered.

'Before I go back to my seat, I would like to say three things: firstly, does our being new creatures mean we should cut ourselves off from others? No. I work in Noah's bakery, and I mingle with everyone. The difference is that I will not partake in anything that will lead me to break the commandments of Abba. Secondly, does our being new creatures mean we will not face the problems and difficulties other human beings are prone to experience? No. My friends here and I face temptations, persecutions, and issues in our lives. The difference is that we can keep panic or fear at bay because we can talk to Abba about anything, and we can have counsel from mature brethren. Lastly, Abba can test your faith to know the choice you have made between Him and the devil, but if you slip, He is merciful to forgive you if you truly repent. Thank you, everybody.'

'Sing again!' the gathering of women shouted. *'Please!'*

Razi hesitated, then gave in to the request of their guests.

Leah felt touched watching all these eager and desperate women. Some of them had been led out by Apostle Andrew and Apostle Bartholomew, leaders of the evangelistic team. She saw the Apostles almost pleading with their guests to settle down and listen to the third speaker. Leah had the impression that they wanted the 'Lord Jesus commodity' before it ran out! Finally, everyone was seated and calm again, and the third speaker came up. Mother Johanna. Leah looked on in admiration, as she was sure many others did. Johanna had a captivating presence. She was gorgeously dressed, but it was her charm coupled with her height and very shapely figure that lent her a stunning look. She did not have the length of hair that she herself or her mother did, but her face drew people in. It mustn't have been hard for her to catch men, Leah mused in her mind. This was Father Jephthah's wife. Her mother had told Levi and herself the stories of all her friends and how each of them had been involved in her life. But listening to how each of these women told their life stories from their own perspectives made it all sound different – and exciting. Their stories had a personal touch which was magnetic. Their stories made her feel more sympathetic and appreciative of what Abba had done in their lives.

She could not wait to hear Mother Johanna's story. Some refreshments were passed around at this stage, but Mother Johanna went straight ahead. 'Good morning, everyone. Shalom.'

'Shalom,' everyone answered.

The way she began took everyone's attention away from the food. 'My mother was an easy woman. She gave herself to any man who would look after her. That was how she had me and my brother Josef – from two different fathers. She sent me to her lover to initiate me into harlotry at the age of twelve. I lost my virginity, with different men using my body for three days. What pained me most then was that I was aiming for a more decent life than that of my mother. I started off at Capernaum and eventually came to Jerusalem and began to amass wealth. I assumed this would be my life forever; I could never foresee that things would turn around. I did not hope for a better life, as I was trying to be the best at the only thing I knew how to do – pleasuring men. I was well paid. I invested in property, lived and ate well, and even though I was an outcast, I thought it didn't matter as I had become wealthy. Well, as you can all see, my life turned around when Mother Biliah and Mother Razi over there talked about Lord Jesus and what believing in Him had done for them.

'So, I was convinced and followed them to see Him. I lost the desire to fornicate. I gave up some of my property to help the poor. I was able to engage in weaving and ministering to the sick, which only Abba must have gifted me with because I had never learned these skills before. With my faith in Lord Jesus, I am here before you all to testify that I am now a new creature. I am no longer a slave to sex or to the desire to pleasure rich men for money or to greed for any material gains. I am now happily married, and I had thought I would never have children because my womb was destroyed by disease, but right now there is a baby growing here!'

Everyone jumped up and clapped for joy, and after they calmed down, she continued. Leah expected her to become emotional, but she seemed stronger. 'To me, the greatest miracles in my life since I placed my faith in Lord Jesus are firstly my ability to forgive my mother and accept her – she too is now a new creature—'

More clapping and joy.

'—And then, the miracle of my husband, Jephthah. Not just the miracle of getting married to him but that he too is now a new creature! It may not sound like a miracle, but this was a man who would never attend the fellowship of the new creatures or the congregation of Jews in the temple. He was not interested in either. There is nothing like you and your spouse having the same mindset about Abba and sharing in your faith. So, my soul is completely restored in joy.'

She paused for a few moments. 'We don't want any of you to feel pressured by the amount of information and life stories you have heard today. By the help of Abba, there will be more gatherings like this. One thing is clear. We were once in darkness like you when we were prostitutes. But Lord Jesus said He was the Way, the Truth, and the Life, and if we followed Him, we would no longer be in darkness. We followed Him, saw the light, and our new life stories are far better than the old ones. This is what we want to share with you today through our stories and songs. It will not be possible to hear everyone's testimony today, but we have a song for you now: *In Times Like These.*'

Leah saw her mother, Mother Razi, Mother Biliah, Mother Amina, and Mother Abigail all go to join Mother Johanna in front. Even Mother Rachel went forward! There were two other women she did not know very well. They held each other's hands, forming an arc in front of their audience. Mother Johanna began, in a clear, steady voice. A lovely voice, but not heady like her mother's or dramatic like Mother Razi's. The rest of the women sang the chorus.

'In times like these, you need a Saviour
In times like these, you need an anchor
Be very sure, be very sure
Your anchor holds and grips the Solid Rock!

This rock is Jesus, the only One
This Rock is Jesus, the only One
Be very sure, be very sure
Be very sure, be very sure
Your anchor holds and grips the Solid Rock!'

After the clapping and cheering, the women went back to their seats while the two Apostles came forward and another round of clapping echoed around the room.

'Shalom, everyone,' Apostle Bartholomew greeted. 'I want to thank the team of women who have designed this programme to bless us. They have witnessed and shown that forgiveness is very important, and that no one can enjoy the peace, freedom, and love of God without forgiving all who have hurt us in one way or the other. Lord Jesus forgave all those who crucified him. Let us all remember that for new creatures, God sends His Holy Spirit through Lord Jesus to help us. We will end this programme by asking Apostle Philip to pray for any woman who has made the choice to live the new life by putting their faith in Lord Jesus Christ. May Abba Father bless and protect you all. Amen.'

Everyone closed their eyes, and Apostle Philip prayed for the gathering of the sixteen women who had turned up. Leah heard him say that the devil had come to steal, kill, and destroy people's happiness, health, families, and lives but Lord Jesus had come so that everyone could have life in abundance and to destroy the works of the devil.

Leah's mind wandered off as she found herself thinking of Father Benjamin's grandson, Moses. He liked her, and she liked him. What should she do about Tim, though? He was obviously smitten by her, but she saw him as a brother, just the way Levi did. She did not feel the same excitement thinking about Tim as she did about Moses, who made her feel conscious of herself in a new way. She suddenly thought about a conversation she'd had with Moses:

'Leah, when will you and Levi come to our Centre?' he said.

'I need to think about that.'

'But I like the idea,' Moses replied.

'You do?' Leah asked, feigning innocence.

'Of course! Can you guess why I pleaded with my parents to let me stay with my grandparents?'

'Oh... tell me. I can't guess why!' Leah squealed with faux naivety. 'Wait a minute... I think I can guess why. It's so you can attend the Dan centre with them.'

'Why would I want to attend the Dan Centre with my grandparents?' Moses asked, looking at her adoringly.

'You like the Dan Centre better than the Bethel Centre, then?' Leah ventured.

'No, Leah! It's so I can get to see you again. Now you can guess why I came to sit with you.'

'To chat with Levi?'

'Honestly, Leah! I didn't realise you're a teaser. Alright, look at my eyes, and then you will know why.'

'Why? What are you talking about?'

'Alright, Leah. I will try a different line. You have a special place in my heart. I am fond of you. It is you I think of all the time – more than all the other girls in Judea. There, I have laid my heart open. Still confused?'

She shook her head. She looked down at her feet, suddenly shy as she realised that his words had helped her understand why she felt self-conscious around him.

She wondered now if she still a new creature, having these kinds of thoughts. She felt guilty as she realised that the prayers and even the announcements were all over.

CHAPTER 19

You must be born again.
John 3:3

That same Saturday morning, at a hotel at Sidon, Apostle Jude, Father Josef and Father Nebo were in the middle of an outreach to eleven male prostitutes. There were nine at the beginning, but two more men had sauntered into the gathering. The evangelistic team from Jerusalem comprised Father Lucas, Father Jephthah, Father Asher, Brother Yosey, Brother Ram, Timothy, Moses, Jesse, Father Nahum (Moses's father) and Levi. After the introductions of the guests to their hosts, some brief testimonies from Yosey and Nebo, and a good meal, the next item on the agenda was Josef's testimony.

'My dear friends, I am Father Josef. I have come to share my testimony so that you can join us to stand for what we now believe is the truth and fight the good fight of faith and become true sons of God. Like me, you will run away from all those sinful things that bring shame and make you outcasts. After you hear my testimony, you will chase a right relationship with God and live a godly life. Then God will keep His promise to rescue you from every trap of the enemy.

'The first time I told someone about my prostitution was to a female prostitute who had always known me as Jocheb. I told her my real name. At this point in my life, I was privileged because my sister Johanna had been talking to me about Lord Jesus, His personality, His miracles – which all of you here have admitted you have heard about. But what was it that really convinced me? Like you heard from Yosey, I was his lover three years ago, but it took that long for him to be convinced because Abba's own plan for his salvation was different from mine. I was not able to convince him until he came to see things for himself about twelve months ago. In my own case, I had the added advantage of my sister, who was one of the followers of Lord Jesus. She would tell me the miracles she witnessed and the Lord's messages. All these were advantages for me. Why did I listen to her or take her seriously? Listen, she had been a seasoned prostitute since the age of twelve. I lived with her as a business partner in Capernaum, attending to clients who preferred me to her. Then, she met Lord Jesus. Her life changed for the better. I witnessed the transformation, and this alone prepared my heart to seek Lord Jesus.

'Many times I tried to engage in other business, get a good woman and settle down, but I couldn't. I was enslaved to male prostitution as the devil brought extremely wealthy clients my way. I invested in brothels and became a landlord of several properties. This was all discreetly done. No one knew. I lived in a grand house and operated a leather factory I established far away from my residence. At night, I went to clients' homes or wherever they wanted us to meet.

'I desired what I saw in my sister's life – Mother Johanna, the wife of our Brother Jephthah here: she was free; she was joyful; she had no more sexual urges – and it did not make her poorer. I followed Lord Jesus and ate His bread, and I suddenly had no desire left for prostitution. I had divine strength to forgive our parents, who had led my sister and I into prostitution. I was introduced into a family of believers of my new faith. I was able to get married, and now I have a three-year-old adopted son and a two-year-old son, and my wife is expecting another miracle in three months' time!'

Loud, hearty cheers and claps greeted this news.

'This is what I want for you all. I would not have come here to expose my soul, but I know what you are all going through. I have been there – the shame, the frustration, and the constant feeling of rejection, and not enjoying true happiness. Some men live a double life. They feel tortured in a loveless marriage because their lust is for a fellow man. How blessed it would be if they were touched by Lord Jesus so that they could enjoy the true love that Abba gives to a couple. I cannot say it all today, as there will always be opportunities to share testimonies. So, before Father Lucas tells his story, I say a big thank you to you all for sacrificing time to attend and I ask Abba to also bless you through my testimony as well. Thank you, everyone.'

Everyone cheered and clapped Josef, then Apostle Jude made his way to the front of the audience and brought Lucas with him. Levi felt a new sense of pride in his father when he was introduced to the gathering and felt the same pride about his mother and siblings too, when they were acknowledged. Lucas spoke about how his marriage had been destroyed for ten years and how God had miraculously restored him to his wife and children. At that point, Levi himself was introduced and warmly applauded.

He was surprised that his father sounded as authoritative as any of the Apostles as he told his story, and he realised he no longer felt ashamed of him. There were many men like him, as evidenced by those who gave testimonies, and there were more who did not have the courage to testify that day.

After his father had told his story and the other testimonies were over, Levi hoped that Apostle Jude would not spend a great deal of time on the prayers; he was particularly renowned for giving long messages and rambling prayers. Levi tried to focus his attention on Jude's words. His father sat beside him and took his right hand, giving it a firm squeeze to affirm his support and love.

Apostle Jude cleared his throat. 'Welcome, everyone, to the Kingdom of God and Heaven – the miraculous! How? Well, this is the world of the new creature, where you decide the miracles that happen in your life when you allow your faith in Abba to enrich your life. For example, where you forgive your family and friends as Lord Jesus forgave all who condemned, tortured, and killed him. You become a light to others. Lord Jesus said we should not keep a lamp under a basket but on the table so that everyone will benefit. This is what this outreach is about: to plant Jesus and His words in your heart so that you hear the truth through revelation by the Holy Spirit of God.

'As you have heard from my friends here, each of them yielded their hearts to the truth. They built their faith on the miracles and works they saw Lord Jesus do before He was crucified. God enabled them to believe that Lord Jesus is the Messiah. May your hearts be like good soil that will take in all that you have heard today so that the seeds of faith will germinate and grow.

'The devil will try to steal your attention, plant doubts, and make you stay in sin. But remember the testimonies you have heard today. Miracles from Abba are for people to experience. It is just like receiving a gift when you work out your salvation with faith. Talk to Abba, and He will send His angels to help you when He sees that you really want to change your heart and depend on Jesus Christ for your salvation.

'Before Lord Jesus came, most Jews went to the synagogue and followed all the Jewish traditions, the Ten Commandments and

God's laws in the Torah and the scriptures. I know that some of you are not sure of what a new creature is or what it is to be born again into the new faith. I will tell you. Some of you might know Rabbi Nicodemus, one of the leaders of the Sanhedrin. He was the one who asked Lord Jesus how a person could find eternal life – how they can go to Heaven. Lord Jesus said to him, 'One must be born again.' He meant the starting of a new life. When you renew your lives and start all over again in the new faith, you become a new creature! You leave behind your past sinful life and move into the new life, where you are not condemned because you have been forgiven by Abba. For a start, you ask Lord Jesus Christ to come into your life and be your saviour. Today, then, my dear friends, is the day to pray that prayer of faith and have the peace of God forever. You see! Salvation is not complicated. Words are powerful. When we speak words, our minds follow what is said. Healing, joy, and numerous blessings are given the opportunity to enter our lives. Supernatural help and divine interventions are also the privileges of the new creature. Let us pray:

'Dear Abba, we have planted Your words in the hearts of Rafael, Mahkai, Ezekiel, Adriel, Eliam, Reul, Haziel, Nima, Dathan, Karmel, and Isaiah. Please loosen their chains, and ensure Your words firmly stay in their hearts so that they may grow towards you. That they will see the truth of Your words and so be granted revelation of who they are in Christ Jesus. We ask that you bind every plan of the enemy to distract them, plant doubt, mislead or steal away all that they have heard today. We also ask that because they came out here as a step of faith and wanted to reach out to You, please meet each of them at the very point of their need so that they too will testify to Your glory like Josef, Nebo, Yosey and Lucas have testified to Your glory. Bless them even as you have blessed all those who testified today. This we ask in the name of our Lord Jesus Christ, Amen.'

'Amen,' everyone said.

'Now, I would like our guests to stand or kneel if they wish to and say after me: *Dear Abba, thank you for sending Lord Jesus to die for my sin. Please forgive me for every wrong I have done and am still doing. From this moment, I will follow Lord Jesus as my Saviour and guide. Please grant me the grace to follow You and to begin to enjoy the blessings You have promised me. I ask all this in Jesus Christ's name, Amen.*'

Apostle Jude allowed silence to fall for a few moments, then said, 'I want you to remember that the days are evil; there is persecution and the scattering of new creatures. But do not forget that when you gather in loyalty, faith, and love, as one body, there is power and strength. You need one another. Never forsake the gathering of the brethren.

'Lord Jesus called me and some of my friends who were fishermen to reach out to others, and we did. He revealed the Truth of God and the Kingdom of Heaven to us, and we came out of darkness. All that we share with you are His messages. This is what we have come here to do today – to introduce you to Lord Jesus and invite you to accept Him as the Messiah. God will make a distinction between you and the people of the world – those who decide to live in sin, even after hearing this good news of Jesus.

'Even when difficulties come, keep the right attitude, and whatever difficulty that was meant for your harm, it will turn out for your good. Your lives as new creatures will be a light to others in darkness. Father Josef here, Father Nebo, Yosey, and many others used to indulge in male prostitution, but today, like you heard, God has blessed them exceedingly since their becoming new creatures. Father Josef, please pray for our friends before I get so carried away.'

Father Josef quickly overcame his sudden surprise and stepped out to lead the prayer of deliverance. He was surprised because he thought this had already been done. It would be his first time leading such a prayer. He modelled his words on the way he had seen Apostle Jude lead prayers during the team's evangelistic outreaches. *'Dear Abba, we thank you that we conquer the enemy by our words of testimony. We bring this message to our friends so that Your truth can be proclaimed...'* He paused for a few seconds. 'Dear friends, I want you all to repeat this prayer if you are willing to become new creatures: *Dear God, thank you for sending Jesus Christ to die in my place. Please forgive me for all that I have done wrong. I will follow You and become a new creature by the power of Your Holy Spirit, in Jesus Christ's name, Amen.'*

'Amen,' chorused all the people present, amidst the rejoicing of the saints and the angels in Heaven.

Apostle Jude beamed. 'Thank you, everyone, for taking time to come out to listen to us. If there is anything you take away from all you have heard from us today, it is this: *There is no condemnation for those who are in Christ Jesus.'*

The devil sent out his chief angels who were usually very successful: Angel Fear, Angel Doubt, and Angel Cynic. They rushed straight to the hearts of all who had heard the messages of the evangelistic teams, planting their corrupting seeds by reminding them of persecutions and the fact that Lord Jesus had not been able to save himself.

At the same time, for every one of His rival's angels, Abba released three to tackle each one. Angels Faith, Hope and Testimony were sent to combat Angel Fear. Angel Praise, Angel Wisdom and Angel Love were sent out to divert Angel Doubt, while Angels Truth, Knowledge and Light tackled Angel Cynic.

In addition, angels from Heaven joined in with a song shared with the prostitutes by both evangelistic teams to bless all who had become new creations of their old selves:

Have you ever said 'YES'?
Have you ever said 'YES'?
Have you ever said 'YES' to Jesus?
Have you ever said 'NO' to the devil and so –
Have you ever said 'YES' to Jesus?

On Calvary's cross, your sins He bore
Don't keep your Lord outside the door
He is waiting to bless in His righteousness;
Won't you now say 'YES' to Jesus?

CHAPTER 20

So it is no longer I who live, but it is Christ who lives in me.
This life that I live now, I live by faith in the Son of God,
who loved me and gave his life for me.
Galatians 2:20

Timothy was excited. Apostle Jude was starting a youth ministry and he had been informed that he, Timothy, would be the pastor in charge! He savoured in his mind how he and his mother had reacted to the news.

'Dear Timothy, the Apostles and the elders like your zeal for the Lord and admire greatly how you conduct yourself. You are an excellent role model for our young people. You did not have the privilege of an earthly father for the first twelve years of your life, yet you have remained close to the Lord and hold your faith in Lord Jesus strongly. I want to ask you if you will be able to pastor the Youth Fellowship?'

He had stared at his mother with an open mouth before facing Apostle Jude. 'I am honoured, sir. With God's help through Lord Jesus and the power of His Holy Spirit, I will do my best.'

As soon as he spoke, his mother embraced him with tears, saying repeatedly, 'My son, my son, you are more than ten sons in one to me. Thank you for bringing me joy and pride!'

'Your answer pleases me, Timothy,' Jude said. 'I know you are very young, but God has blessed you with wisdom and leadership qualities. We have noticed that even your peers respect you. You will have helpers, of course, whom you will choose to assist you, but you will be in charge. How old are you, again?'

'Thirteen, sir.'

'That is impressive. The Youth Fellowship will be held here in your home, and it will be called the Timothy Centre. It will be for youths only. For now, let it run on Saturdays for just thirty minutes to an hour at the most. This news will be announced in all the centres during their fellowship this week, but it will not start until next month. The other Apostles and I will meet with you from time to time to discuss how you are getting on. Let us pray over it…'

This was just two days ago. Even Levi had not heard the good news yet. Tim could not wait to share it with his brother and friend. He spoke to his mother. 'Mother, do you need anything? I would like to visit Levi and tell him the good news.'

'I understand how you feel, my son, but Levi will hear the good news on Wednesday during their fellowship. You know how dangerous the times are. We must not be seen to ignore the warnings of the Apostles. Walking on your own is unsafe, considering what has been happening to followers of our Lord Jesus. As a leader of youths, you should show a good example. We can fellowship in his home in two days' time, and you can tell him then.'

'What would be the point? It would be announced. How about you take a stroll with me? It is just about twenty minutes' walk. Please, Mother,' he pleaded.

Adah looked at her son. If she had been wealthy, she would have got him a gift. At least she could oblige him this simple request. 'Alright, son. I really don't feel like taking a stroll, and your stepfather is away too, but the fact that you have been appointed a youth pastor gives me the desire to please you.'

'Thanks so much, Mother. Let's go!'

'Not immediately, Tim. I have to dress up, even though it is just a stroll.'

The evening weather was perfect. It was cool, and it felt great to breathe in the refreshing air. There were lots of people about, some strolling like they were and others pursuing their business.

'So, Pastor Timothy, how do you feel about this new role placed on your shoulders? Don't you feel nervous about it?'

Tim smiled. 'Never, Mother. I am so excited, happy, and eager to start. Can you imagine that other boys my age and older were bypassed, even though some of them have richer parents or have parents who are highly placed in our community?'

'Exactly. I was very surprised too. Mother Rachel will be so proud of you.'

'I know… but there is someone in particular who I'm sure will be proud.' Timothy beamed.

'Of course – Father Josef!'

'Yes, he would be… but that is not who I had in mind.'

'Oh, then who?'

'Um… Leah.'

'Oh!' his mother said, surprised.

Timothy's face took on a darker look. 'Although… she seems to have more respect for others who have fathers or come from wealthier homes than myself.'

'Did she tell you this?' his mother said gently.

'No, but she told Levi that I am just like a brother to her when she knows I have feelings for her.'

'Oh, I see. I know you have feelings for her, and you assumed she had feelings for you as well. So, who has she eyes for?'

'Maybe Moses, maybe Jesse. I don't want to know.'

'Moses is another very responsible young man like you. He is fourteen. He was already a year old when I had you. You know what, son? Just as this new role has come to you, the same thing will happen regarding whoever God wants you to be with.'

'I don't want anyone else, Mother.'

'Then tell Abba. Such things are out of my control.' Adah stopped and touched her son's arm. 'We have reached their home, son. Please don't take too long. I don't like walking out when it is getting late. Please give them the good news, and after about ten minutes we can begin our return journey home. Come and fetch me. I will be with Eliana.'

'Deal, Mother. Thank you so much for strolling with me.'

OLUSOLA SOPHIA ANYANWU

Epilogue

You have made known to me the path of life;
You will fill me with joy in Your presence,
with eternal pleasures at Your right hand.
Psalm 16:11

The New Creatures grew in number and strength even in the face of persecution. They continued to meet in house fellowship, supporting one another in their faith and reaching out to the outcasts, the poor, the sick, and all who were marginalised in their society. They spread the good news of Lord Jesus as the Way, the Truth, and the Life, and the path to God the Father in Heaven.

Many became missionaries as they went to other cities outside Judea in Europe, Asia, and Africa. There, they nurtured and prepared the hearts of people and planted the seeds of faith in their hearts.

Abba God blessed the works of their hands and encouraged them through His Holy Spirit as they used the name of Jesus Christ to defeat the plans of the devil in their lives.

BIBLIOGRAPHY

New Testament and Psalms Bible
KJV Bible
NLT Bible
NIV Bible
Message Bible
Songs of Praise hymn
Joyce Meyer's Bible
Good News Bible
Scripture Union Choruses – 5 Wigmore Street, London, WIH OAD
I have decided to follow Jesus by Sadhu Sundar Singh [1889-1929]

ABOUT THE AUTHOR

Olusola Sophia Anyanwu is British Nigerian. She did all her schooling in Nigeria and trained as an English and Literature teacher. She relocated to the UK in 2003 and has continued as an educationist. She is a best-selling author and a poet who has enjoyed reading and writing from childhood. Her father, Chief Augustus Adebayo, was also a famous published author and introduced her to the world of books, encouraging her and her siblings to the culture of enjoying stories. Sophia is a reviewer, encourager and believes in inspiring people through her writing to imbibe the love of God and derive encouragement. Sophia is a member of the Association of Christian Writers, UK TRELLIS Poetry Group [Facebook], Alliance of Independent Authors, Society of Authors and worships at Emmanuel Baptist Church, Thamesmead.

www.ingramcontent.com/pod-product-compliance
Lightning Source LLC
Chambersburg PA
CBHW051648040426
42446CB00009B/1028